Problems of Modern Music

NORTON LIBRARY EDITIONS

Edited by Paul Henry Lang

THE CREATIVE WORLD OF MOZART

PROBLEMS OF MODERN MUSIC

STRAVINSKY: A NEW APPRAISAL OF HIS MUSIC

PROBLEMS
of
MODERN MUSIC

The Princeton Seminar
in Advanced Musical Studies

Edited by Paul Henry Lang

W · W · NORTON & COMPANY · INC · *New York*

The essays in this book first appeared in the April 1960 issue of *The Musical Quarterly*.

FIRST PUBLISHED IN THE NORTON LIBRARY 1962

Published simultaneously in the Dominion of Canada by George J. McLeod Limited, Toronto

W. W. Norton & Company, Inc. is the publisher of current or forthcoming books on music by Gerald Abraham, William Austin, Anthony Baines, Sol Berkowitz, Friedrich Blume, Howard Boatwright, Nadia Boulanger, Nathan Broder, Manfred Bukofzer, John Castellini, John Clough, Doda Conrad, Aaron Copland, Hans David, Paul Des Marais, Otto Erich Deutsch, Frederick Dorian, Alfred Einstein, Gabriel Fontrier, Karl Geiringer, Harold Gleason, Richard Franko Goldman, Peter Gradenwitz, Donald Jay Grout, F. L. Harrison, A. J. B. Hutchings, Charles Ives, Leo Kraft, Paul Henry Lang, Jens Peter Larsen, Maurice Lieberman, Joseph Machlis, W. T. Marrocco, Arthur Mendel, William J. Mitchell, Douglas Moore, Carl Parrish, John F. Ohl, Vincent Persichetti, Marc Pincherle, Walter Piston, Gustave Reese, Curt Sachs, Adolfo Salazar, Arnold Schoenberg, Denis Stevens, Oliver Strunk, Francis Toye, Donald R. Wakeling, Bruno Walter, and J. A. Westrup.

PRINTED IN THE UNITED STATES OF AMERICA

3 4 5 6 7 8 9 0

CONTENTS

INTRODUCTION

THE Parisian master architect, Jean Mignot, overseeing the building of the cathedral in Milan in 1398, declared *Ars sine scientia nihil.* This was in answer to an opinion then beginning to take shape, that *scientia est unum, et ars aliud.* For Mignot, the rhetoric of building involved a truth to be expressed in the work itself, while others had begun to think, as we now think, of houses, and even of God's house, only in terms of construction and effect. Mignot's *scientia* cannot have meant simply engineering, for in those days engineering was considered an art, not a science; his *scientia* meant *ratio,* the theme, content, or burden (*gravitas*) of the work to be done, and was not concerned with its functioning or with the esthetic satisfaction it might provide. And so, too, for music. Guido d'Arezzo's words, *Nam qui canit quod non sapit, diffinitur bestia,* are strong words. Many centuries have elapsed since these views were widely shared, but something of this sort is once more in the air as the age-old and omnipresent strife between old and new is reaching a particularly acute stage, in fact, a stage that has few parallels in the history of music. "This is no longer music"— the popular rallying slogan, is quite familiar to the historian, but while such an attitude has often obscured progress for a generation or two, it has never caused such an upheaval and such weakening of artistic integrity as during the last two generations. To make a comprehensive analysis of the situation is a Herculean task and will call for much more serious and judicious effort than the rather wild pamphleteering that goes on in European periodicals, though here and there one sees very respectable studies.

Feeling the necessity for clarification, Princeton University with the enlightened help of the Fromm Foundation last summer organized a Seminar in Advanced Musical Studies. This great university thus proudly reaffirms that music is indeed an integral part of the history of ideas, a concept so sadly lacking in the music departments of most of our institutions of higher learning. In its turn, *The Musical Quarterly* is proudly reaffirming its own traditions of furthering musical thought by publishing the main papers of the Seminar. Many of our readers, like ourselves, are concerned by the new developments in music, knocking on the doors of a new world without finding the handle that would gain them admittance. We believe that these papers offer guidance and enlightenment and that they make for profitable reading. The general conclusions of a productive assembly, which make up in strenuous thinking what they lack in length and elaboration, are here summed up. The reader will be interested to observe the tone of the various contributors. There is the calm, reasoning, and forbearing musician who, knowing that changes are necessary and inevitable, examines all phenomena with care and with an open mind. Then there is the defender of the new faith to whom the new can come only at the expense of the old; the *weltfremd* thinker; and the man who just tags along. But the aggregate is enlightening and permits us an insight into the inspirations and aspirations that govern musical thought at the beginning of the seventh decade of the 20th century. We recommend that the reader place a *da capo* sign on Roger Sessions's introductory essay, to which he should return after reading the last article. It contains many well-reasoned observations, but we should like to single out one that may serve as a *cantus firmus* whenever the going gets rough: "A conscientious artist, if genuinely adventurous, will accept anything whatever only strictly on his own terms."

* *
*

By way of introduction we may sketch in the background from which this mid-century stock-taking grew, and perhaps add a few comments of our own.

The first half of the 20th century passed under the sign of violent antitheses. First there was revolutionary dissolution, followed by severe, tradition-oriented concentration; emphatic subjectivity, then dogged objectivity and studied collectivism, The same extremes can be detected in the constituent featu-es of music. Form became so fragmented that its dangling remnants could hardly be detected, but subsequently it solidified, triumphantly rediscovering age-old esthetic tenets — and then petrified.

Melody, in the post-Impressionistic world, became a color patch, an exclamation, the smooth surface of its face ruined by the varicose veins of incessant chromaticism. Then there developed a desire for broad design, diatonicism, folk tunes in the old ecclesiastic modes, even pentatonic melodies, only to be succeeded by "rows." The tonal system, already showing ambiguities in *Tristan,* disintegrated, then the aimlessly floating harmonic clouds were blown away, and "atonality" was subjected to military discipline. We have seen how the Niebelung orchestra was later dwarfed, only to be followed by a new *da camera* concept.

Then came the great reckoning with affective functions of music. *Verklärte Nacht* still billowed with Tristanesque vapors in orgiastic abandonment, but Stravinsky declared that feelings and passions do not exist in music, only in the listener's imagination. Music should be nothing but an autonomous order of sound progressions, ruled by the logic of construction, for music cannot express anything but itself. Unfortunately, while impersonality can be a powerful weapon against romantic exuberance, it can serve also as effective camouflage of artistic irresponsibility; the neo-Classic sewing-machine counterpoint rattles along with unfailing precision, for a motor is impersonal. And so is the gesture when purely geometrical, and so are the sound track, the electronic instruments, and the *Sprechgesang*. The champions of objectivity made even the Baroque impersonal, regimenting its revived counterpoint so that it could be used as a mask behind which they might hide. The whole of this new objectivity is nothing but a mask. From this *cul de sac* there was no way out, only a radical change of course could extricate the composer.

At first Impressionism seemed to be the only durable movement, the only style capable of preserving European traditions, because in essence neither Debussy nor his disciples and imitators broke the old frames, they merely loosened them. They did find many new colors and made the orchestra even more dazzling, the result being that Ravel, Dukas, Delius, Falla, even the American Griffes, are still welcome to subscription audiences as "modern" composers. As a matter of fact, some of our justly admired brilliant and slick orchestras were built to cope with this very style. But this is a hothouse art that needs artificial heating, and by the time Ravel died the school was so destitute of substance that the much-admired composer of *Daphnis et Chloé* was reduced to orchestrating Mussorgsky. All of them sought exotic subjects and themes, for they felt that Europe's Impressionistic pomp needed colonies to replenish its color resources. Delius turned to the Appalachians, Roussel and Holst to Indian lore, and so forth. Others rediscovered folksong, and English,

Irish, Jewish, and American folk tunes invaded their music. But gradually musicians became satiated with the winter garden of Impressionism and began to rebel. It is characteristic that the leaders of the anti-Impressionist movement came from its very core: Satie, Milhaud, Honegger, Stravinsky. All of them began as Impressionists, it was only later that they struck out in other directions. It was obvious that the Impressionism of the early century had to be outgrown, very much as had the Rococo of the mid-18th century.

But what lay ahead of the rebels? One by one they began to realize that by leaving the sheltering haven of hedonism they would be isolated, and of that many were afraid. Still, there were quite a few composers who did not shrink from solitude, who indeed sought it; some belligerently, some with ascetic devotion. Among them were several of our own composers who could not be shaken in their determination to go their own way, and to them it did not matter what the others tried to do, for all of them shared Mr. Sessions's motto to which we have referred.

The central figure of the movement that led to the dissolution of the order was Schoenberg, who began where the fifty-year-old Strauss was to end. *Gurrelieder* was the last monument of gigantism; then Schoenberg suddenly turned around, abandoned the immense apparatus, and devoted himself to intimate chamber music. His Second String Quartet is the symbolic marker of the road that was to lead from Wagner to Bartók. But he did not follow that road, for to him and his disciples, all of them accustomed to wallowing in Tristanesque emotionalism, the most urgent task became the undressing of music in order to rid themselves of its gaudy garments. They wanted the naked body of music; distilled, test-tube truth.

Tonal order and logic was the chief guardian of sensuousness, therefore it had to be eliminated. While others, like Hindemith, Stravinsky, and Bartók, also assaulted the old order, they never really abandoned it altogether; but Schoenberg firmly believed that he represented the will of the age when he eliminated it by declaring all twelve tones of the octave to be of equal, sovereign significance. There still remained the innate sensuousness of the singing voice which, too, had to be destroyed and changed into speech-song. Schoenberg turned out to be a real, inspired leader compared to whom Satie, Cocteau, and their kind were only artistic playboys. His school was so strong and influential that it compelled obeisance in all lands. One by one the coryphées declared their fealty. We have witnessed the most abject surrender only recently, when Stravinsky, always aloof, arrogant, used to command, bared his head before "the three Viennese," obediently accepting terms. His magnificent pagan colors and blood-boiling rhythms that once were the admiration of every musician are gone and he, too, writes "objective" serial music, cold, grim, and beautifully made.

We have arrived, then, at a stage where we see two extremes locked in contest. We have some able and independent composers, no longer young but seasoned in wisdom and experience, who believe that one can still contribute new interests without completely forswearing old ones. They are anything but mossbacks, the Hindemiths, Sessionses, Carters, and all the others; they are perfectly willing to experiment and learn, but they believe that where there is not even a semblance of tradition every convention is inartistic, every stylization a form of academicism. Total serialization they regard indeed as a new form of academicism, incredible as this may seem to the revolutionary switchboard artist.

At the other extreme we have a very vocal segment of the new generation to whom all that is left of two millennia of music is its physical components, which are manipulated with the aid of electronics, stop watch, and slide rule. Therewith begins an inevitable tendency, a rapprochement to the physico-mathematical, which changes Mignot's still somewhat flexible dictum into the unequivocal *ars nihil sed scientia.* Even the thoroughly artistic and esthetically fruitful twelve-tone system is no longer acceptable. Our readers will notice that reference is several times made in these articles to "the classical twelve-tone technique," that is, Webern has already been relegated to history. They have gone far beyond the old, once dreaded method of "composing with twelve tones," and are now in the world of total serialism in which every aspect of music, not only pitch succession, is governed by "premeditation."

Once more we wish to state that the historian and critic must never be impatient even when faced with the seemingly fundamental negation of everything that has passed before. He remembers Galilei's *Dialogo* and similar devastating manifestos, and he knows that some good will undoubtedly emerge from this latest upheaval. But he also remembers what Bury said, that history "is in the last resort somebody's image of the past, and the image is conditioned by the mind and experience of the person who forms it." Therefore our comments, though honest and carefully weighed, are of necessity based on that possibly frail and biased mind and experience. It is regrettable that this is not given some recognition, or at least the courtesy of the benefit of the doubt.

When Friedrich Blume in a thoughtful and eminently fair recent article attempted to find an answer to the recurring question "What Is

Music?" as seen by an independent, historically schooled observer from the perspective of the far slope of the 20th century, the government of the *avant garde,* represented by *Melos,* immediately ordered total mobilization. A special issue of the magazine was ordered into the battle line, reservists were recalled to the colors, though some of them were manifestly over age as far as present-day music is concerned. The fusillade was impressive, main and secondary batteries all firing armor-piercing shells, but the gunnery was poorly directed and Mr. Blume was not even straddled. This is a deplorable reaction, reminding us of the Parisian censor's immortal words when he banned Méhul's opera, *Mélidore:* "It is not enough that a work is not *against* us, it must be *for* us." Our readers will find none of this attitude in the Princeton papers. The authors who appear in these pages are responsible and devoted musical thinkers who respect the venerable tradition of free inquiry, which is the sole premise acceptable to a great university and also to a periodical such as ours.

* *
*

Total serialization was bound to create a feeling of incarceration, and even among its adherents a certain uneasiness is manifested in this regard. As Mr. Krenek so succinctly states: "Invariancy inherent by definition to the concept of the series . . . leads to uniformity of configuration that eliminates the last traces of unpredictability." Pierre Boulez, also disturbed by the problem, puts it very nicely when he says: "The unexpected, again: there is no creation except in the unforseeable becoming necessary." This makes sense; after all, it was always the essence of great music, and the mark of genius, to do the unexpected instead of the routine. But the remedy proposed by the total serialists is anathema to any esthetic system known to us: "the factor of chance." Regrettably, the justification of the "element of chance" leads to some very slipshod philosophizing. It is comfortably likened to what is traditionally considered "inspiration." But to Mr. Krenek inspiration is a treacherous thing, it is influenced, nay, "dictated," by tradition, training, and experience, none of which can be trusted, therefore the duty of a truly advanced composer is to set up an "impersonal mechanism" and then bedevil its premeditated patterns with elements of chance. Now Edward T. Cone, whose paper is a model of open-minded progressivism, professional competence, and just plain healthy musicianship, avers that when chance is invoked as an element of construction, logic is largely inoperative. He detects the same limitations in strictly enforced serialism, for in either case he finds that the music can be explained only by referring to "an external structure." We are afraid that Mr. Krenek, able and shrewd as he is, falters at the end of his article. Sooner or later, of course, he had to face the inevitable question of "the expressive or communicative aspects of music." But how can moods and feelings be serialized? Indeed, we may ask with Mr. Sessions, how can rhythm, tempo, and dynamics be serialized? Mr. Krenek does not "exclude the possibility" of total serialism being or becoming "a medium of some sort of communication," but we are afraid that this slight concession makes as little sense as his last sentence, in which he intimates that this communication "may mean as much or as little as life itself."

Mr. Krenek somewhat diffidently states that "whatever morphological kinship may be detected between adjacent sections [in his *Circle, Chain, and Mirror*] . . . is a consequence of the premeditated serial arrangement . . . and not dictated by requirements of a so-called musical nature." A startling statement, this, and surely the most contemptuous utterance in the present anthology. It surprises coming from a musician, and a good one, who once basked in the "so-called" music of Mahler; but then converts are usually more zealous than the pope. Mr. Cone thinks that these despised musical requirements are not yet buried, that in a more generalized form, the compositional values of past centuries are still cogent and viable. This is certainly borne out by at least two distinguished composers represented in this issue: Roger Sessions and Elliott Carter. It seems to us that what Mr. Cone offers in this regard makes far more sense. He calls it a "crucial" point, and, indeed, it is nothing less. "A work of art ought to imply the standards by which it demands to be judged." This is a principle that is often ignored and often violated by the American-Legion-like professional patriotic organization of serialists. Luigi Dallapiccola, for whom we have great admiration as a composer, gives the dodecaphonic accolade to — Mozart; and Allen Forte, in one of the articles appearing in this issue, offers a good-conduct medal to Bartók. Mr. Forte finds in the Hungarian composer's Fourth String Quartet "the extended and elaborate expression of a relational system that closely resembles a serial schema." Though the author immediately adds that "the system upon which it is based arises as a logical consequence of tonal materials unique to the Fourth Quartet," he proceeds to deduce serial significance from the work. Still, he must operate with requirements of a "so-called musical nature" which, apparently, are not welcomed by the purists. What is it that Mr. Krenek wishes to substitute for this awareness of morphological kinship?

We are aware that we are aware, and can even inspect the content of our awareness, but hardly the act of awareness itself.

A special warning is in order concerning Milton Babbitt's contribution. The language and symbolism by which he strives to communicate the subtle distractions of an uncompromisingly honest and incisive spirit convinced that it has found a whole, may seem eccentric, obscure, and prolix. But the reader should remember that Mr. Babbitt, a fine musician, is also an eminent mathematician, and he speaks here in mathematical terms of the implications of "a permutational musical system as opposed to the combinational system of the past." In mathematics there is no emotion, no feeling; it is the supreme and only certainty that man can achieve. Mathematics is the music of the intellect, a happy abstract world where there is no need for a knowledge of life, for mathematics does not know the incomprehensible complications of life. And how much simpler it is than life! It is relatively easy to understand the axioms of Euclid, but the minute we begin to moralize, and thus turn to life, things become infinitely complicated and difficult to understand. We do not profess to be able to follow Mr. Babbitt's disquisition beyond a very modest degree, but since it comes from an unquestionably competent and dispassionate source, and has undoubted relevance to the problems under discussion, it will prove enlightening to those versed in the mathematical systems presented, which are absolutely beyond the ken of the Editor of this journal.

Now we come to the executors of the mathematical theories, the musicians who carry out empirically the postulates of which Mr. Babbitt speaks. Vladimir Ussachevsky tells us how he composes for the tape recorder, a bright, versatile, obedient, but soulless instrument. The process is very involved and bears as little resemblance as possible to what one innocently supposes to be the course of musical composition, whether tonal or serial. The electronic composer has a bank where he deposits sounds for further use. When withdrawn, the sounds are put through various operations, they are filtered, split, spliced, enriched, thinned, etc. The next steps are interesting. A given musical material is re-recorded at different speed. The new pitch levels so created are then synchronized with the original, thus creating Mr. Krenek's "unpredictable" by purely mechanical manipulation. All this looks pretty forbidding, but Mr. Ussachevsky, whose paper is altogether free of the boasting so characteristic of his engineer-musician colleagues, says with earnest and convincing simplicity that he now "habitually imagines a sound as if it were changed by the [various] mutation techniques." That is, he can imagine the pitch variations caused by different tape speeds, in fact, can imagine the sound even when it is played backward. Nevertheless, his description of the composition of a tape recorder piece, while interesting and informative, only attests to the experiments of an inquisitive mind. He believes in what he does but refrains from promising the coming of the kingdom of the electronic tube on earth.

It seems to us that with electronic music we have arrived at a critical conflict of concepts not well understood by either scientist or musician. It is agreed that we possess a three-dimensional tonal space which, expressed in greatly simplified terms, is made up of the duration of the sounds, their arrangement in pitches, and their intensity. But there is a decisive difference between mathematical-physical hypotheses of the theoretical tonal space and the actual effects of music as an art. This is where the electronic composers and their scientist supporters are gravely in error, for they create a false relationship between acoustics and music, between objective nature and subjective art. In justice, we must mention that they look back upon a respectable ancestry. The Pythagoreans held that the mathematical ratios between tones are identical with the basic conditions of music, but in reality we are dealing here only with a psychophysical parallelism. That the Pythagorean doctrine is debatable was already recognized by Aristotle and Aristoxenus, who granted the musician what Mr. Krenek denies him: the right of *aisthesis,* that is, the right to his own feelings and interpretations as opposed to the calculations of the Pythagoreans. Much later, the able and outspoken Mattheson thundered against the acousticians who presumed to dictate to the artist. Today, the scientist and engineer no longer presumes to dictate to the artist, he and his machines take over the artist's role and métier, lock, stock, barrel, and ramrod. The opposition of such men as Mattheson rests on the fundamental difference between mathematical-objective tone and musical-subjective tone, and on the difference between physical and esthetic pitch, and finally, on that between acoustical and psychical dynamics. Therefore the three-dimensional tonal space just mentioned is nothing but a bit of science fiction, whereas musical procedures with their human conditions are far more complicated, irrational, and metaphysical.

Perhaps the first person in modern times to attempt to derive the phenomena of music from physical conditions was Goethe, who liked to concern himself with everything. He got some questionable advice from his court musician, Zelter, a very minor composer and therefore an avid theorist and critic. Then later in the century there were two great scholars, Helmholtz and Stumpf, whose very valuable contributions to the science of acoustics and psychology of tone made the acoustic-physiological-psychological approach to music a firmly established discipline. But neither they nor the more recent mathematical scientists really understood music, only the *materia musica*. For the core of the musical process, of the creative process in music, is subject neither to physics, physiology, nor mathematics, but is an artistic thought process, a musical logic, virtually independent of the natural sciences. We are not dealing with physics but with music, not with science but with art; it is the human element that is decisive. No matter how earnestly the scientist tries to fix standards, the true musician will never accept them unconditionally. Our friends of the electronic tube claim that civilization has finally progressed so far as to make possible the creation of an absolutely pure and correct tone synthetically, by electricity. They even have the temerity (witness Dr. Olson) to dismiss the Stradivari violin as useless because it produces "impurities" on account of the fallibility of the human finger and the scraping of the bow. Why, it is precisely in these human frailties, in this expressive impurity, that life and humanity are revealed. A totally aseptic tone produced by machines will be a dreadful thing.

Well, the reader is earnestly bidden to read these interesting essays attentively and with an open mind. But when he has digested their portent he might remember that man, the musician — and not the physicist and the mathematician — is the measure of all music making. Aribo beautifully expressed this in the 11th century, when he said that one must wonder at the grace of God when observing the lowly minstrels who without the slightest idea of the theories and doctrines of music play "entirely correctly."

P. H. L.

PREFACE

THE Seminar in Advanced Musical Studies grew out of the same concern with the realities and necessities of American musical life that has motivated all the activities of the Fromm Music Foundation. Our efforts have never been intended to be patronage in the old sense of comprehensive support of a segment of musical activity or a group of artists, but rather a series of stimulants that should focus attention, by their example, upon the most promising aspects of creative activity.

One of the serious problems in our musical culture has been the frustrating isolation of young composers and performers from each other, which is intensified by the often unsympathetic attitude of performers towards the music of our own time. Although this situation has been abundantly recognized, most attempts at alleviation have been diffuse and sporadic. We therefore determined to begin our own efforts in this direction with a concentrated experiment. For its testing ground we chose the Berkshire Music School at Tanglewood, since this school is a center for students from a wide geographical area who converge upon it each year for a brief period of intense musical activity. Aaron Copland accepted our invitation to head this Tanglewood project, beginning in 1957.

To meet the many challenges arising from the gulf between the creative and re-creative elements in our musical culture, the Fromm Fellow Players, a group of eleven young performers distinguished by their skill, integrity, and eagerness, was formed. One of their responsibilities was to assist the composition department in resolving problems that can be best demonstrated in performance. They also performed at the weekly lecture-concerts honoring visiting and resident composers, gave carefully rehearsed performances of student works at the Composers' Forums, and appeared in two formal concerts of 20th-century music. Contemporary music thus became a more significant part of the Tanglewood scene and the basis of a new and lively interaction between composers and performers. Imbued with a growing awareness of and enthusiasm for the contemporary spirit, each player returned home prepared to set off a cultural chain-reaction.

During my visits to the Berkshires I met with composers and performers to discuss ways in which the Tanglewood experience might bear upon other areas in our musical culture. In the course of these discussions our attention was drawn, again and again, to the plight of the loneliest individuals in contemporary music — the young professional composers. Advanced beyond "instruction," they are aware of musical problems and eager to come to grips with them. Their expectations of acceptance by society, raised by the fellowships and prizes available to them as students, prove unfounded; while at the same time they have lost the stimulating contact with their fellow-students that enriched their school days. These composers are young people to whom Schoenberg, Webern, and Berg are no longer objects of controversy but pioneers of the early 20th century. Although they are aware of everything that really is contemporary, they have no one with whom to share this awareness. Their chances of entry into public musical life have been barred by the insurmountable barrier of their own originality and the hostility of individuals and institutions who deny the public anything that cannot be standardized.

We talked of the European seminars at Darmstadt and Donaueschingen, where discussion of common problems lessens this feeling of isolation, and where contact with masters of the older generation helps the younger people find their own directions. Out of the conviction that Americans need no longer depend upon Europe for their resources, we decided to propose to Princeton University the establishment of a seminar for study, on the highest level, of the most significant trends in contemporary musical thought. Here all contemporary doctrines could be freely examined, stressing above all the primacy of musical experience and imagination, and categorically distinguishing artistic production from systematic thought. In this way we hoped to give the young professional musicians a rallying point, an assurance of inclusion in our musical culture.

Roger Sessions, who as a composer and teacher occupies a most distinguished position in the musical world, was a natural choice as director of the seminar. All his creative life Sessions has lived and composed in serene solitude, relying only on self-criticism and mature artistic judgment to determine his creative objectives, without regard for public approbation or criticism. Thus he stands now as an inspiring example of dedication to his art.

The faculty that joined Mr. Sessions at the first Seminar included Milton Babbitt, Edward T. Cone, Robert Craft, and Ernst Krenek. The seven guest lecturers who contributed to the high level of the Seminar were: Elliott Carter, Aaron Copland, Allen Forte, Felix Greissle, John Tukey, Vladimir Ussachevsky, and Edgard Varèse.

The Seminar was also honored by a visit from Igor Stravinsky, who spoke informally to the participants.

The members of the Lenox Quartet, who were in Princeton as seminarists and musicians-in-residence, presented three programs of contemporary music which included, besides works of the composer members of the faculty, works by Bartók, Bloch, Kirchner, Schuller, and Webern.

Twenty-five musicians of professional status, averaging about thirty years of age, were selected for participation in the Seminar from the large number recommended by leading musicians throughout the country. They took part in fifteen hours of weekly lectures and discussions. The substance of the proceedings may be found in the articles that follow.

A few imperfections led us to modifications in our plans for future seminars. Discussions of performance problems seemed over-generalized when divorced from actual experience. We recognized that too much oral discussion can be frustrating for musicians to whom musical notes communicate ideas more genuinely and directly. Consequently, we have evolved a new pattern, which will be applied for the first time in 1960.

Greater diversity as well as greater integration will characterize the 1960 Seminar. Regular seminars will again be given by the staff, this time consisting of Messrs. Sessions, Babbitt, and Kim, of the Princeton faculty, as well as two guest composers, Elliott Carter and Karl Birger-Blomdahl (Sweden). All eleven Fromm Fellow Players (woodwind quintet, string quartet, soprano, piano) will also be on hand, and will spend each afternoon rehearsing new music. This music will be chosen by the faculty from works by members of the seminar, not in terms of a competition or a symposium, but solely on the basis of the presentation of problems of general interest. The composers involved will lead the rehearsals in the presence of the members of the seminar and of one faculty member, who will function as a moderator. This should stimulate a spontaneous cross-fertilization between composer and performer, through which each should gain insights into the problems and objectives of the other. It is to be expected, moreover, that important subjects arising during these afternoons will be singled out by the moderator for fuller elaboration in the more formal morning seminars. The guest lecturers will be encouraged to emphasize areas not included in the regular curriculum, which will bring about an even fuller integration of the total plan.

If our ideas can be realized, the Princeton Seminar in Advanced Musical Studies will become a force in our musical culture, a positive indication that serious artistry need not be compromised even in a society in which creative achievement is generally less recognized than material success. Our young composers will carry home with them a sense of rededication, a new strength born of the knowledge that the creative potential of man is inexhaustible.

PROBLEMS AND ISSUES FACING THE COMPOSER TODAY

By ROGER SESSIONS

THE premises behind such an undertaking as was attempted in last summer's Princeton Seminar in Advanced Musical Studies were of course based on the obvious changes in orientation and outlook that are taking place—and have for many years been taking place—in the minds, attitudes, and intentions of the composers, performers, and even listeners of our day. It is hardly necessary to point out in these pages that change is inevitable at any period whatever in the development of an art. The history of the art is itself primarily an account of such changes and an attempt to fathom both their wide-ranging causes and their equally far-reaching effects, and to formulate terms in which these can be adequately grasped. The History of Art likewise seeks and provides criteria by which the main periods of change may be compared with one another in character and extent.

The history of Western music reveals at least two phases, and possibly three, that may well have seemed to those who observed them as contemporaries to shake the art of music to its depths and to raise questions of the most fundamental kind—questions, that is, not only as to the character and trend of current developments, but as to the function, the significance, and even the ultimate nature of music itself. The beginnings of polyphony, the late 16th and early 17th century, and possibly the 13th and 14th—if this be not indeed considered as a late phase of the first-named—were such phases. They were periods of apparent crisis, during which long-established values were brought into deep question and challenged both on the most profound and the most superficial levels; "experimental" periods in the sense that many things were tried which soon proved abortive, while others, soon discarded, seemed to find justification at a much later date; but periods of intense creativity not only by virtue of the music of genius that survived them, but because they tapped new veins, uncovering the resources out of which the music of the following three or four centuries was to be built. In each period the musical transformation was coeval with a far-reaching transformation in Western society, and undoubtedly related to it, though the exact nature of this relationship seems—at least to this writer—far more difficult to penetrate and to clarify than it is frequently assumed to be.

The period in which we live has at the very least much in common with these earlier ones. For well over a hundred years each successive generation has seemed to many of its members to contain within itself the seeds of the imminent destruction, not only of a great musical tradition, but possibly of music itself. Though this had happened at earlier periods also, it has happened at a steadily increasing tempo since, roughly, the death of Beethoven. Each generation has, to be sure, at length become assimilated, by and large, to the "main stream"; the "revolutions" have in each case been discovered eventually to be not so revolutionary after all, and the revolutionaries of one generation have become symbols of conservatism and eventually clubs with which to beat their revolutionary successors of the next. But, with each succeeding phase, this has come about a little more slowly, and there is no doubt an easily discernible reason for this. It is true that in our time the situation of all the arts, and in all of their phases, has been rendered far more complex, first through the development of mass media, and the consequent immeasurable expansion of the more-or-less interested public, and secondly through various economic factors, including not only the decline of private patronage and the consequent and inevitable increase in commercialization, but drastically rising costs in virtually every phase of musical production. It is however no less true that, precisely at this moment of economic and, if you will, social crisis in the arts, the inner dynamic of music itself should be leading to developments of which the eventual result can at best be only dimly sensed.

One symptom—or result—of this, of course, may be seen in the increasing articulateness of musicians themselves in regard to their own artistic principles. Since the early years of the 19th century composers have felt more and more inclined to express themselves in print regarding music and all of its phases. In the case of earlier composers—Mozart and Beethoven, for instance—one must rely on correspondence, on reminiscences, and on a few sybilline and perhaps problematic quotations that have become traditional, and no doubt often distorted, if one wants to discover their working principles beyond the evidence of the music itself. From Carl Maria von Weber on, however, composers have devoted considerable effort and energy to criticism, later to theory, and more recently still to teaching. This is certainly due in very large part to the fact that, in a period of artistic upheaval, creative artists find themselves first of all sharply aware of their own relationship to their traditional inheritance and to the directions in which they feel impelled to extend or even to reject it. Secondly, they find themselves, in a period in which the formulated notions regarding musical esthetics, musical theory, and musical syntax have long since lost the vitality they once possessed, impelled or even obliged to arrive at what are at least working formulations of their own. If they are not to remain in relative solitude they are also likely to communicate these formulations. Since the cultural pessimism of our time abhors solitude—once considered a decidedly honorable state for an artist—and demands "news" at almost any price, they may even find themselves virtually compelled to do so.

One has only to open practically any European periodical devoted to living music in order to become aware of the intellectual ferment that characterizes the musical life of today. One will find there, as one finds in fact on all hands, serious and often acute discussion of every phase, from generalized esthetic attitudes to the most precise and esoteric matters, and on a level that the conscientious artist of mature age, or the ambitious one of more tender years, cannot wholly ignore except at the price of an inherent lack of adventurousness which in itself bodes somewhat ill for his achievement as an artist. I of course do not mean to imply by this that he is bound to accept all or even any of the ideas he will find urged upon him. If he is genuinely adventurous he will accept anything whatever only strictly on his own terms. But he will find himself, certainly, challenged at every point, and obliged to find his own answer to the challenges thus presented to him; and if he is young and gifted he will welcome these challenges as a test of his creative conviction, if not as a source of direct stimulation along the lines of his own expression. At the very least, he will have the opportunity to become more aware of his own musical nature, and at the best he will learn to be untiring in his effort to avail himself of that opportunity, and to pursue his own creative efforts accordingly.

That the situation as I have described it contains its own peculiar pitfalls is, of course, obvious. I am not referring to the comment one frequently hears to the effect that a period in which musicians think and talk so much about their art must necessarily be a sterile one. As a matter of fact the present-day habit of drawing broad inferences of such a kind — apparently plausible but inherently far-fetched — is one against which we should guard ourselves in the name of elementary logic. It is not my purpose here, however, to propose value judgments on contemporary music, but merely to comment on facts and phenomena as they exist. But the least one can do is to point out that contemporary music, and in fact any music whatever, is to be judged in terms of music itself, not of circumstances with which no clear connection can be convincingly demonstrated. One cannot insist too strongly or too frequently that, in the arts generally and in music in particular, it is only productions that really count, and that only in these — music, written or performed — are to be found the criteria by which ideas about music, as well as music itself, must finally stand or fall: not the converse. This is a refrain that will recur repeatedly in the course of this discussion, as indeed it must in the course of any valid discussion of music.

The generic pitfall at which I have hinted is precisely this one. In an age in which theoretical speculation in either the esthetic or the technical sphere has assumed the importance it has in our own, there is always the danger that it may be over-valued, and assumed to furnish criteria in itself, and not regarded simply as a means that may prove useful in helping composers to achieve the artistic results they are seeking — in the realization, that is, of a genuine musical vision. Again, one finds oneself obliged to emphasize that the primary function of the composer is to possess, develop, and with the utmost intensity to realize his own particular vision — a vision which, if it is genuinely vital, will be found to contain both general and specifically personal elements; and that theory and esthetics can have validity for him only in so far as they can find roots in this vision. Otherwise they can represent only a flight away from music, or at a very dubious best, a crutch on which a faltering musical impulse can find some measure of support.

It is in fact fairly easy to recognize the pitfalls characteristic of those past musical periods with which we are most familiar. To a certain extent they are mirrored in the way in which these periods are regarded by the succeeding generations, which rebel against them. The characteristic pitfall of the 19th century was undoubtedly that of literary association and the manner of over-emphasis—sentimental, violent, or pretentious—just as that of the 18th was a certain type of elegant and formal conventionality. Our own particular brand of emptiness is perhaps beginning to emerge in a variety of clichés, derived both from so-called neo-Classicism and from serialism in its earlier as well as its later phases. In each case we are dealing with a manner that has become generalized through lack of substance, and not with ideas in any positive sense. What is necessary, if the pitfalls are to be avoided, is that composers in the first place should always retain the courage of their own artistic vision, that teachers should emphasize the supremacy of real musical imagination, and that listeners, of whatever category, should, by holding themselves open to whatever genuine and even unexpected experience music can bring, learn to discriminate between what is authentic and what is fictitious.

Thus far I have spoken at length of a general situation in the musical world, and of some of the questions that situation raises as such, without attempting to deal with the situation itself, its background, or its nature, other than to characterize it in the very generalized sense of the decay of one tradition and the gradual movement towards new factors capable of superseding it. The ultimate shape these developments will assume is still by no means definitive in its outlines; but both their causes and their present trends are in certain respects quite clear, as are the specific questions posed by the latter.

It seems clear, for example, that the development of harmony as we have traditionally conceived it has probably reached a dead end. First of all, composers have for many years felt able to utilize all possible vertical combinations of tones, and have so abundantly availed themselves of that possibility that any new discoveries in this regard are virtually unthinkable. Even this fact, however, tells only a part of the story, since the possibilities are not so rich as this purely statistical assumption would indicate. As more and more tones are added to any chord, each added tone contributes less to the character of the chord, or, in other words, to the factor that differentiates it from other combinations of tones. The decisive development of harmony, therefore, depends overwhelmingly on combinations of a relatively small number of tones; beyond that number, so to speak, the ear refuses to interest itself in strictly harmonic effect. It is not so much a question of possibilities as such, as of possibilities that are in any way decisive. The real point is that composers seem by and large no longer interested in chords as such, and that this is a tacit recognition that there is nothing left to be discovered, in the sphere of harmony, that arouses any feeling of excitement on their part.

Something similar had of course taken place already in regard to functional harmony. Based very clearly on a triadic premise, the principle of root progression had given way before the proliferation of "altered chords" that was so characteristic a feature of harmonic evolution in the 19th century. The process is a perfectly familiar one which need not be summarized here. Suffice it to say that what is often called "atonality" was a very gradual development—so gradual, in fact, that, aside from the literal meaning of the term itself, it is impossible to define with any precision whatever. It is in other words impossible to show exactly where tonality ends and "atonality" begins unless one establish wholly arbitrary lines of demarcation in advance.

This is not the main objection to the term, however. "Atonality" implies music in which not only is the element of what is defined as "tonality" no longer a principle of construction, but in which the composer deliberately avoids all procedures capable of evoking "tonal" associations. Actually this is virtually impossible, owing to the mere fact that we use tones, and hear them in relation to each other. In other words, whenever a series of tones is heard, the musical ear assimilates it by perceiving a pattern composed not only of tones but of intervals; and neither the process nor the sensation is different in any essential principle from the process by which one assimilates music that is unimpeachably "tonal." I am reliably informed that Anton Webern himself insisted on this point, and even on specifically tonal references in his own music.

Whatever real sense the word "atonality" may have derives from the fact that the further a chord departs from a strictly triadic structure, the less unequivocal it becomes in terms of a specific key; and that, in the proportion that such harmonies become predominant in musical usage, it becomes more difficult to establish genuine tonal contrast, and the effort to do so becomes more forced. As the cadence, in the early years of this century, came to acquire for composers more and more the aspect of a cliché, and as the composers found themselves more and more obliged to discover other means of achieving musical articulation, they found themselves obliged to discover new principles of contrast as well. They discovered that in the absence of strictly triadic harmony it was virtually impossible to establish a feeling of key sufficiently unequivocally to make possible a genuine and definitive change of key, and that hence tonality was for them no longer sufficient as a principle of structure. It was this discovery perhaps above all that led to both the adoption of the serial principle by Schoenberg and the attempt to find ways towards the revitalization of tonal principles that was embodied in the "neo-Classicism" of Stravinsky.

The above does not mean, of course, that harmony has ceased to exist in any music, or that it has become an element that can be ignored. Our harmonic sense is essentially the awareness of one of the dimensions of music; having acquired that awareness, we cannot do away with it, and it would be ridiculous folly to try to do so. If art is to develop, awareness of every aspect of the art must increase rather than diminish. But harmonic effect as such has clearly ceased to be a major interest of composers, just as tonality has ceased to be an issue or a point of reference against which issues can be adequately discussed. To be sure, the question still arises constantly in the public discussion of music; but such discussion can have no meaning except on the level of very precise technical definition. We are dealing with facts, not with slogans, and the facts have to be referred to basic esthetic and acoustical considerations, rather than to specific historical embodiments of these. If by "tonality" we mean, in the most general terms, the sense of pitch-relationship and of the patterns and structures that can be created out of such relationships, the word "atonality" can have no meaning, as long as we use tones. If we mean, on the other hand, a precise set of technical principles and hence of procedures, it is easy to see in retrospect that the very vitality with which it developed led ultimately beyond the principle itself.

If the cadence, as conventionally defined, came finally to seem to many composers, in the context of their own music, little more than a cliché, it was because they came to feel a definite disparity between the harmonic vocabulary native to them and the harmonies necessary to establish the cadence. While the composers of the late 19th century —one senses the problem already in the music of Wagner—succeeded in overcoming this disparity, often through sheer technical ingenuity and sometimes with visible effort, their successors often found this impossible to achieve without stylistic violence. It was necessary either to turn backward or to seek new principles.

As we all know, a similar development took place in the rhythmic sphere. It took place more quietly and with far less opposition, if indeed there was any appreciable opposition whatever. There is no need to dwell on the rhythmic question here. Though the changes that have taken place have been equally far-reaching, they have been in a sense less spectacular and less esoteric, if only for the reason that they owe so much to the influence of popular music and of Gregorian Chant. They have found incomparably more ready acceptance, both from musicians and from the general public, than the developments of which I have spoken in the realm of harmony. Furthermore, the rhythmic aspects of music are bound closely and inevitably to the other elements of the musical vocabulary; in this sense one can say that the development of music away from the tonal and cadential principle has also created a whole new set of rhythmic premises and requirements.

In any event, the focal point of the more advanced musical thought of today is polyphonic, and more concerned with problems of texture and organization than with harmony in the hitherto accepted meaning of the term. Once more, this does not mean that composers have ceased to be acutely aware of vertical relationships between tones, of progressions from one vertical conglomerate to another, or even of the patterns formed by such progressions. But it is certainly true, I think, that they tend more and more to think of these matters in terms of texture rather than harmony as hitherto defined. The current trend is to refer to such vertical conglomerates as "densities" rather than as "chords" or "harmonies"; but it must be stressed that there is no satisfactory substitute for awareness of the entire musical context, and that the replacement of one term by another is useful in so far as it increases that awareness, and does not connote the evasion of one issue in favor of another.

It is of course fashionable to regard Webern as the patron saint of the dominant contemporary trend, and to invoke his name as a rallying point for all that is most aggressively anti-traditional in contemporary music. As is so apt to be the case, there is a discrepancy at many points between Webern the symbol and Webern the actual figure. The latter, however individual his musical style, was of course as deeply rooted in the Viennese tradition as Schoenberg himself, and probably more narrowly; and without in any sense meaning to detract from his musical stature, one can say that he remained a loyal disciple to the extent of being more Schoenbergian than Schoenberg himself. In the last analysis he was at least as much the Romantic Expressionist as Alban Berg, if not more so. Above all, and most important, he was a musician of the ripest culture, at once the most daring and the most realistic of artists. The teacher who at times finds himself obliged to stress the fact—so easily lost from view in the heat of speculative enthusiasm—that musical values are, first and last, derived from tones and rhythms and the effects they produce, and not from their theoretical consistency or analytical plausibility, can find no better or more demonstrable evidence in his own behalf than that furnished by almost any score of Webern.

At the same time, however, one may find oneself impelled to question the sufficiency of the post-Webernian trend as a firm and comprehensive basis for new departures in music. This brings us to the large question of serialism, which I have deliberately postponed till after discussing some of the factors that have given rise to it. One cannot, of course, stress too much that serialism is neither the arbitrary nor the rigid set of prescriptions that it is often supposed to be, not only by its foes but unfortunately also by some of its friends. It is rather the result of many converging trends of musical development, of which I have mentioned a couple of the most important and the most general ones. Above all, perhaps, it is the result of the decreasing validity of the harmonic principle as an organizing force, and the necessity of adopting consistent relationships between tones, which can serve as a constructive basis for the organization of musical ideas, along both the horizontal and the vertical dimensions.

Quite as important is to stress that serialism is in full process of development, and that the shapes it has taken are already manifold. It is no longer the exclusive possession of any one "school" or group of composers, nor is it bound to any one mode of expression, Viennese or otherwise. Need one cite evidences, at this date? In other words, it is a technical principle that a wide number and variety of composers have found useful for their own purposes, both because of the organizing principles they have derived from it and because of the musical resources it has opened up for them. Like any other technical principle, it yields nothing in itself; it is always for the imagination of the composer to discover what it can give him, and to mold it to his own uses. Like any other technical principle, it has to be thoroughly mastered, in terms of the composer's creative vision; a half-baked relationship to it in this respect can produce only less than half-baked results. For this reason the young composer who has not grown up with it from the beginning—there are already a number who have done so, and to whom it is, so to speak, native—would be well-advised to avoid it until he has become sure of his own musical identity, and can grow into it in full conviction and genuine musical maturity. It does not provide answers to all musical questions or in the last analysis to any; it is only a vehicle and a means, which, let us reiterate, many composers find useful. Once more like other technical principles, it has acquired its own brand—several brands, in fact—of academicism, and many varieties of cliché, which are none the less recognizable as clichés for being derived from a technical principle that has been in active existence for little more than forty years. Its value lies wholly in the music of the composers who have seen fit to adopt it, and the value of that music resides in the imaginative, emotive, and constructive force inherent in it, not in the ingenuities with which the system is applied, except in so far as these are the inherent result of a musical conception.

The serial organization of tones must be, and for the most part is, today regarded as a settled fact—the composer is free to take it or leave it, or to adopt it with varying degrees of rigor, as he may choose. The results it can yield are open to all to see and judge as they see fit. More problematical are some attempts that have been made to extend serial organization to other aspects of music—notably to that of rhythmic values and that of dynamics. Any discussion of these matters must emphasize once more that it is only results that matter; that the human imagination works along channels that are frequently unexpected, and that a critical scrutiny of technical premises does not release one in the slightest degree from the responsibility of holding one's mind, ear, and heart open to whatever may reveal genuinely new vistas of musical expression and experience.

With this caution in mind one can easily observe that tones are, for the musical ear, fixed and readily identifiable points in musical space, and that the progress from one tone to another has a clear point of departure and arrival. This is partly the result of the fact that within the octave there are only twelve tones, with which the musical ear has familiarized itself over the course of many centuries; and the additional fact that our musical culture has taught us to regard as equivalent tones that occupy the same position within the various octaves. A, for instance, is recognizable as A whether it be played on the open A string of the double-bass, of the 'cello, or of the violin—or, for that matter, in the high register of the flute or the piccolo. Time values, on the other hand, are by no means fixed; their range is to all intents and purposes infinite. This does not at all exclude the possibility of adopting an arbitrary series of time values for the purposes of any single composition, but it does raise very valid questions regarding the serialization of time values as a general principle. The serialization of dynamics, however, raises questions of a much more fundamental nature. Dynamic values are by their very essence relative, both in an objective and a subjective sense. They have quite different meanings for different media and under different conditions.

How can we regard as equivalent, except on the most practical level of balance, a given nuance on, say, the oboe and the violin, or for that matter, the same nuance in different registers of the same instrument; or on the same note on the same instrument, sounded in a small room, a large concert hall, and the open air? What does the indication *p* actually mean, and how can we as listeners distinguish in clear terms a transition from *mf* to *f*, or even from *mp* to *ff*?

The basic question of all is of course—as is often the case—"Why?" The principle of so-called "total organization" raises many questions and answers none, even in theory. First of all, what is being organized, and according to what criterion? Is it not rather a matter of organizing, not music itself, but various facets of music, each independently and on its own terms or at best according to a set of arbitrarily conceived and ultimately quite irrelevant rules of association? Was the music of Beethoven, or who you will, not totally organized in a sense that is much more real, since it is an organization of musical ideas and not of artificially abstracted elements?

The subject of "total organization" leads naturally to the consideration of electronic media, since the latter make possible the exact control of all musical elements, and make possible in a sense also a partial answer to some of the questions I have raised. Since the potentialities of electronic media in the realm of sound are, at least to all intents and purposes, infinite, it is possible to measure all musical elements in terms of exact quantity, and in fact necessary to do so, since such measurement is the very nature of the instruments and the method by which they are used. A dynamic nuance thus not only can, but must, become a fixed quantity, as can and must, also, any tone in the whole range of pitch or color gradations. Every moment of music not only can but must be the result of the minutest calculation, and the composer for the first time has the whole world of sound at his disposal.

That electronic media will play a vital and possibly even decisive role in the future of music is not to be doubted. I must confess however to skepticism as to what that precise role will be. Two questions seem to me to be crucial. First of all, it is not sufficient to have the whole world at one's disposal—the very infinitude of possibilities cancels out possibilities, as it were, until limitations are discovered. No doubt the limitations are there, and if not there they are certainly in human beings. But the musical media we know thus far derive their whole character and their usefulness as musical media precisely from their limitations—stringed instruments derive their character and utility from not only the fact that they are stringed instruments, that the tone is produced by stroking strings, but from the fact that they are not wind or percussion instruments; and we have learned to use them with great subtlety of effect and power of expression because of that. The dilemma of electronic musical media is a little like that of the psychologist who is reputed once to have said to one of his friends, "Well I have got my boy to the point where I can condition him for anything I want. What shall I condition him for?"

The other question has to do with the essential nature of music itself. Is music simply a matter of tones and rhythmic patterns, or in the final analysis the organization of time in terms of human gesture and movement? The final question regarding all music that is mechanically reproduced seems to be bound up with the fact that our active sense of time is dependent in large degree on our sense of movement, and that mechanical repetition mitigates and finally destroys this sense of movement in any given instance; it destroys also our sense of expression through movement, which plays so large and obvious a part in our musical experience. This is what lies behind the discussions of the element of "chance," which has so bothered the proponents of "total organization." But the element that "total organization" leaves out of account is not chance at all. It is the organic nature of movement as such, of the fresh and autonomous energy with which the performer invests each musical phrase, every time he sings or plays it, and which gradually disappears for our awareness if we listen so often to a mechanical reproduction of it that we become completely familiar with it, to the point of knowing always exactly what is coming next. It is more than the element of mere "surprise"; it is rather that if the expression of movement is to become effective, we require not only the evidence of movement from one point to the next, but a sense of the motivating energy behind it.

To raise these questions is not in any sense to reject the principle of electronic music as such. In the first place, composers are beginning to feel the need for new instruments. The existing ones, for all their technical perfection, are beginning at times to seem vaguely obsolete as far as some of the composers' musical ideas are concerned. The possibilities electronic music suggests are altogether likely to make this situation more acute.

In my own opinion, electronic media more than justify their existence if only by the new insight one can gain from them into the nature of sound, musical and otherwise, and above all by a vast quantity of fresh experience they can provide, on the purely acoustical level. They are still in a clearly very primitive stage and it is impossible to say what they may contribute in the future. But they raise the above questions and many others, and the questions will certainly become more acute as the media develop.

One hears a good deal, these days, of the developing "dehumanization" of music and the other arts; and specifically in regard to the tendencies we discussed in detail at the Princeton Seminar last year, and which I have been discussing in these pages. This is all very well, and not without its plausibility; but we are speaking of a movement that is widespread among the younger composers of Europe, that has begun to take root in the United States, and that above all is in constant development and evolution. Many ideas are being tested, and many are quickly discarded. If we regard certain manifestations with raised eyebrows, that is our privilege as members of an older generation, as it is always our privilege to point out flaws in logic. But if it is also our prerogative to insist on the primacy of the creative imagination, and to minimize the decisive importance of theoretical speculation, we are at the same time obliged to abide by our own premises, and look towards artistic results rather than towards the ideas by which these are rationalized. By the same token it is well to remember that art, considered on the most objective level, reflects the attitudes of the individuals that produce it. The danger of dehumanization is a real and patent one, and the individual can, and certainly should, resist any dehumanizing tendency with all his strength. But this cannot, and must not, blind us to the claims of whatever is genuinely new and vital in the arts, or, once more, cause us to forget that it is the product, not the process, that is of real importance; and that the creative imagination, at its most vital, has revealed himself through many and often surprising channels. There is no reason to believe that it will not continue to do so, as long as creative vitality—which for musicians means above all the intense love of music—continues to persist.

ANALYSIS TODAY

By EDWARD T. CONE

THE analysis of music—especially of traditional music—is one of the most respected of theoretical disciplines, but the respect in which it is held would do it a disservice if it prevented the periodic re-evaluation of the subject. What is analysis, or what ought it to be? What are its purposes? To what extent are traditional concepts and methods applicable to new music? What are the relations of analysis to performance and to criticism? My title refers to a discussion, from the point of view of today, of these questions; it is in no way meant to imply that I have a new system to promulgate, or that I have made startling discoveries about new music.

I

Rather than presenting at the outset a naked definition of the term under consideration, let us begin by looking at a familiar example. The first few measures of *Tristan* have performed many services other than their original one of opening a music-drama; let them serve yet another and open the argument here.

Ex. 1

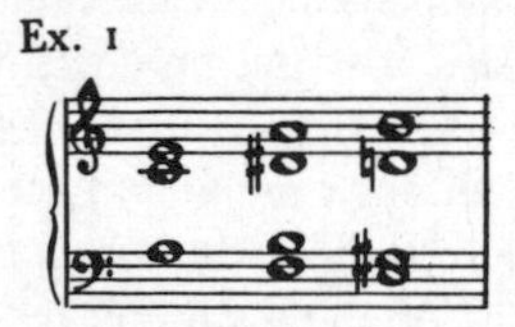

This chordal sequence can be accurately enough described as a minor triad on A, a French sixth on F, and a primary seventh on E; but such a description, revealing nothing of the relationships among the three chords, involves no analysis whatsoever. If, however, one refers to the passage as $\mathrm{I}{}^{5}_{3}\text{-}\mathrm{II}\begin{smallmatrix}\sharp 6\\ 4\\ 3\end{smallmatrix}\text{-}\mathrm{V}{}^{7}_{\sharp}$, he has performed an elementary analytical act: he has related each of the chords to a tonic, and hence to one another. He has made a discovery, or at least a preliminary hypothesis to be tested by its fruitfulness in leading to further discovery. But the analysis as such ceases with the choice of the tonic; once this has been made, the assignment of degree numbers to the chords is pure description. If, on the other hand, one points out that the second chord stands in a quasi-dominant relation to the third, he is doing more than simply assigning names or numbers: he is again discovering and explaining relationships.

Ex. 2

Turning now to the actual score, the analyst might begin a program note thus: "The rising leap of the 'cellos from A to F is succeeded by a chromatic descent, followed in turn by . . ." He need not continue; this is pure description. But when he points out that Example 1 represents the chordal skeleton of Example 2, he is once more on the right track. He can go still further by showing that all the appoggiaturas have half-step resolutions, and that the motif so created is augmented in the motion of the bass, and paralleled in the alto, in such a way that the chordal progression of measures 2-3 becomes an amplification of the melodic half-step of measure 1.

Ex. 3

The fact that in the above diagram no such analogy has been pointed out in the half-steps E-D♯ and A-A♯ is in itself an important though negative part of the analysis, since it implies by omission that these progressions, if relevant at all, are incidental and subordinate.

Going one step further, one might claim that, from a serial point of view, the opening sixth is imitated in the third E-G♯ (see Ex. 4). This is the point at which analysis proper passes over into what I call

Ex. 4

prescription: the insistence upon the validity of relationships not supported by the text. In the above case, for example, the orchestration implies the wrong-headedness of the suggestion, since the opening interval, played by the 'cellos alone, is heard as a unit, whereas the E-G♯ is divided disparately between 'cellos and oboe.

Analysis, then, exists precariously between description and prescription, and it is reason for concern that the latter two are not always easy to recognize. Description is current today in the form of twelve-tone counting—necessary, no doubt, as preliminary to further investigation, but involving no musical discrimination whatsoever. Prescription, on the other hand, is obvious in the absurd irrelevancies of Werker's analyses of Bach but is equally inherent in some of Schenker's more dogmatic pronouncements and in those of his followers.

It should be clear at this point that true analysis works through and for the ear. The greatest analysts (like Schenker at his best) are those with the keenest ears; their insights reveal how a piece of music should be heard, which in turn implies how it should be played. An analysis is a direction for a performance.

In order to explain how a given musical event should be heard, one must show why it occurs: what preceding events have made it necessary or appropriate, towards what later events its function is to lead. The composition must be revealed as an organic temporal unity, to be sure, but as a unity perceptible only gradually as one moment flows to the next, each contributing both to the forward motion and to the total effect. What is often referred to as musical logic comprises just these relationships of each event to its predecessors and to its successors, as well as to the whole. The job of analysis is to uncover them explicitly, but they are implicitly revealed in every good performance. Description, restricted to detailing what happens, fails to explain why. Prescription offers its own explanation, referring to an externally imposed scheme rather than to the actual course of the music.

One more familiar example may clarify this view of logical — or, as I prefer to call them, teleological — relationships.

The recapitulation of the Prestissimo from Beethoven's Sonata Op. 109 bursts in upon the development in such a way that the II♯ (V of V) is followed immediately by I. From a narrowly descriptive point of view one could call this an ellipsis, pointing out that the normally expected V

Ex. 5

has been omitted. Looking ahead, however, one will find that the first phrase of the recapitulation ends on V, and its consequent on I. The puzzling II♯, then, only temporarily and apparently resolved by what immediately follows it, actually points ahead in such a way that the whole passage is bound together in a cadential II-V-I. The propulsion thus generated is given an extra spurt by the compressed II-V-I at the end of the consequent, and the forward motion is renewed with fresh energy by the elision that sets the next period going.

Ex. 6

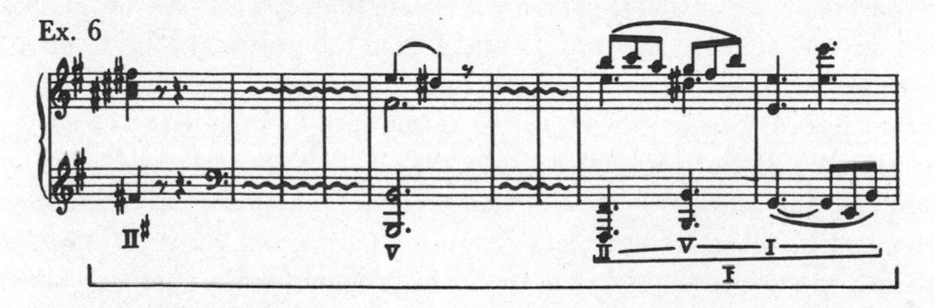

I need hardly mention the obvious effects of such an analysis on the performance of this passage. Whatever doubts one had as to the proper placing of the main accent in these phrases when they first appeared can now be resolved; the exposition can be reinterpreted, if need be, in the new light of the recapitulation.

II

It should be apparent at this point that analysis — and hence performance as it has been discussed above — cannot apply to certain types of composition in vogue today. When chance plays the major role in the writing of a work, as in Cage's *Music for Piano 21-52,* logic as defined above can take only an accidental part. The same is true of music written according to a strictly predetermined constructivistic scheme, such as Boulez's *Structures.* In neither case can any musical event be linked organically with those that precede and those that follow; it can be explained only by referring to an external structure — in the one case the laws of chance and in the other the predetermined plan. The connections are mechanistic rather than teleological: no event has any purpose — each is there only because it has to be there. In a word, this music is composed prescriptively, and the only possible or appropriate analytic method is to determine the original prescriptive plan. This is not analysis but cryptanalysis — the discovery of the key according to which a cipher or code was constructed. (If we are lucky, the composer or one of his initiates will spare us a lot of hard work by supplying us with the key.)

A third category that does not permit analysis is represented by Stockhausen's *Klavierstück XI,* where improvisation is given such free rein that it actually creates the form of the work anew at each performance. Thus *Klavierstück XI* does not exist as a single composition and cannot fruitfully be treated as one. Each new rendition can be discussed on its own merits, to be sure; but the relationship of all such versions to the abstract idea of the piece as a whole, and the decision as to the esthetic value of such an experiment — these problems can be argued endlessly. At any rate they are far afield from the practical considerations that are our concern here. (It need hardly be pointed out that improvisation as traditionally applied to the framework of a Baroque concerto, for example, had purposes quite different. A cadenza served not only to show off the soloist's virtuosity but also to punctuate an important cadence; the soloist's elaboration of a previously stated orchestral melody clarified the dualism inherent in the form. The quality of a given realization depended on its appropriateness to the compositional situation; the performance did not, as in many present-day examples, create the situation.)

III

The analysis of music of the periods closely preceding our own — the 18th and 19th centuries — has almost always assumed the applicability of certain familiar norms: tonally conditioned melody and harmony, periodic rhythmic structure on a regular metrical basis. Naturally such standards cannot be applied uncritically to the music of our own century, but on the other hand they should not be dismissed without examination. I contend that, in a more generalized form, they are still useful. Regardless of vocabulary, linear and chordal progressions still show striking analogies to older tonal procedures, analogies that are in turn reinforced by rhythmic structure. Only in those rare cases where the music tries to deny the principle of progression (as in the examples cited in the immediately preceding section) are such analogies completely lacking.

This point of view is more generally accepted with regard to harmony than to melody, perhaps because harmonic analysis is the more firmly entrenched discipline. After all, for many musicians theory is synonymous with harmony, melody being supposedly a free creative element, neither in its composition nor in its perception subjected to rule. (They forget, of course, that the object of the study of counterpoint is primarily the construction, and only secondarily the combination, of melodies.) Whereas Hindemith's enlargement of traditional harmony to encompass present-day vocabularies is generally known and often applauded, his attempt to find a melodic framework, actually a much less questionable procedure, is often ignored.

Another reason for shunning melodic analysis is that it is not always easy or even advisable to abstract the purely linear element from a progression. Wagner, in such motifs as the *Wanderer* and the *Magic Sleep,* is writing passages in which the melodic aspect is an incidental result of the chordal motion. A little later, Debussy offers examples (like the opening of *Reflets dans l'eau*) in which a linear phrase is dissolved into an atmospherically dispersed harmony that implies without actually stating the expected melodic resolution. Hyper-impressionistic pages, like parts of the *Night-Sounds* from Bartók's *Out-of-Doors* Suite, fragmentize the melody to such an extent that the progressive element is heard to be the increase and decrease of density as the motifs follow one upon the other, rather than the specifically linear aspect, which is here reduced to a minimum. Nevertheless, wherever there are successive differentiations in pitch there is melody of some kind, and wherever there is melody the ear will try to hear it in the simplest possible way.

This is not meant to imply that we must expect to find behind contemporary melodic lines the simple stepwise diatonic framework that Schenker has pointed out in Classical examples. But the ear will naturally connect each tone with those nearest it in pitch. The adjacent pitches may be diatonic or they may be chromatic; they may be actually adjacent or displaced by one or more octaves; they may be present by implication only. In some cases motivic associations or peculiar scale-formations may enforce the acceptance of a larger module — as in the simple case of bugle-calls, the adjacent tones of which are a third or a fourth apart. (In the case of microtonal music, smaller modules may be in effect, although it is doubtful to what extent even present-day ears can accept them.) In every case the ear will do the best it can with the available intervals. It is the duty of the analyst to show the pattern of connections by which an educated ear — his own — makes sense of the total melodic flow.

Even less than in traditional melodies must one assume that there is one uniquely correct way of hearing. Rather, the best analysis is the one that recognizes various levels functioning simultaneously, as when a tone resolves once in the immediate context but turns out to have a different goal in the long run. Two very brief examples may help to clarify this point of view.

Ex. 7

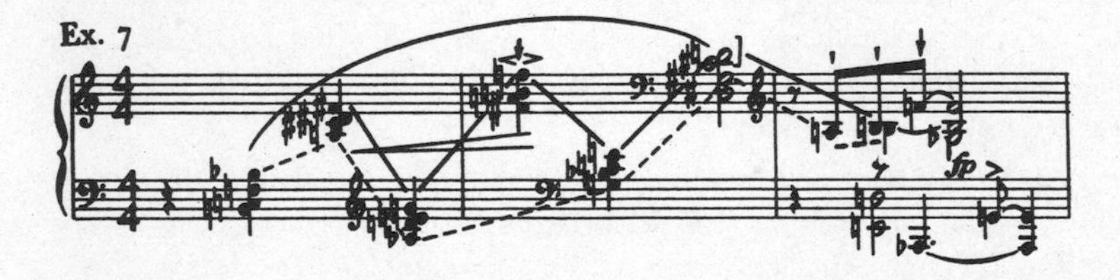

The first is the opening of Schoenberg's *Klavierstück* Op. 33a. Chordal rather than melodic in conception, its linear structure is nevertheless clear. Despite the octave displacements, a line can be traced in the uppermost voice from the F♯ in the first measure to the B in the third. (Notice, however, that at one point two adjacent tones are presented simultaneously instead of successively.) At the same time, the original B♭ leads, through various voices but always at the original octave-level, to the same tone of resolution. At this point the entrance of the F, repeating the climactic F of the second measure, begins a new motion that is carried forward through the succeeding phrase.

Ex. 8

The second passage is from the second of Sessions's piano pieces *From My Diary.*[1] Here both the F in the first measure and the G♭ in the third are associated with upper and lower chromatic neighboring tones. But what of the cadential motif? Why is the pattern altered? And why is the linear descent from the C♭ in the second measure broken at this point? There are several possible answers, all of which are probably relevant. First of all, the most prominent bass-note in each of the four measures — as indicated by its repetition and by its quarter-stem — is an F, which can be heard as a resolution, at another level, of the hanging G♭ — a resolution confirmed by a direct G♭-F in the bass. But at the same time, there seems to be an implied E filling the space between the G♭ and the D in its own voice — a tone suggested by the original association of E with G♭, and by the prominent whole-step motion in the melodic descent. In this case the line gradually increases its pace as it descends.

Ex. 9

But if it seems far-fetched to introduce an unstated, understood element, one can hear the skip G♭-D as a way of emphasizing the cadence, and point out that the motif of neighboring tones aims each time more directly towards its resolution: the first time the neighbors follow the principal; the second time they precede it; and the last time the principal takes the place of one of its own neighbors. Finally, it should be noted that the next phrase takes off from the dangling G♭ in a subtle motivic reference to the beginning.

Ex. 10

It is of course impossible to do justice here to the role of such details in the total melodic structure, but on examination one will find

[1] Copyright 1947 by Edward B. Marks Corporation. Reproduced by permission.

the same kind of connection at work in the large. Note, for example, how much of the first theme of the Schoenberg piano piece is controlled by the high F already mentioned — whether in its original octave or in another — and by its association with the adjacent E. It is again this F, in its highest register, that prepares for the recapitulation; and it is the E that, returning first with the tranquil second theme, later closes the motion in a lower octave in the final measure. In sum, modern melody can not get rid of stepwise motion, because that is the way we hear melody; but it can and does expand (or on occasion contract) the distance, both temporal and spatial, between successive steps. From this point of view even Webern is found to be no pointillist, but a draughtsman of subtle and fragile lines.

The role of harmony in the music of our century, although more extensively explored, is perhaps more difficult, complicated as it is by many factors, such as the frequent exploitation of the static, sensuous effect of the chord in addition to or even at the expense of its progressive functions. As a result, one can no longer assume the easily defined functionality of obviously tonal music. Chords can no longer be precisely named, nor can their identity be maintained in differing contexts. But it is important to realize that, even in stubbornly non-triadic music, the concept of the chord remains, by analogy at least. The composer can set up arbitrary simultaneities that, by their commanding position or by repetition, are accepted as the controlling sonorities — the chords — against which other tones can function in the manner of traditional non-harmonic tones. Bartók's *Improvisations* Op. 20 show how by such a technique quite complicated sonorities can be used to harmonize simple modal folk-tunes. In the following example from the last of Sessions's *Diary* pieces the metrical position and the half-step resolutions suggest that the first chord is an appoggiatura to the second; this supposition is confirmed by the appearance of the root-like D in the bass, and by the clinching repetitions that ensue.

Ex. 11

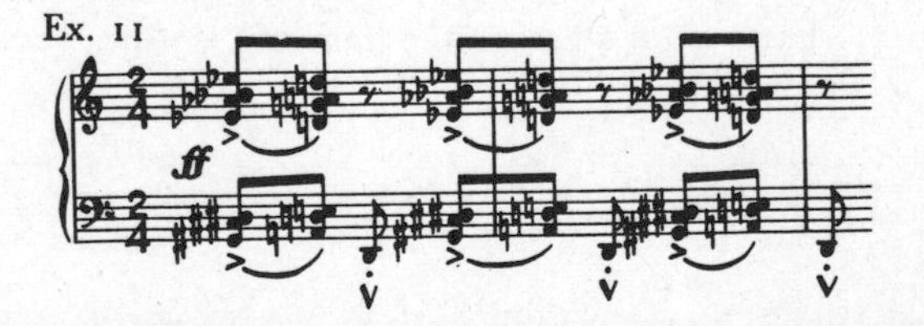

In fact, only where the contrapuntal aspect becomes so strong that every element of each sonority is heard primarily as a point in a moving line, or at the other extreme, where the texture is completely pointillistic, is the chordal concept seriously challenged. In such cases one further assumption of traditional harmony that must then be questioned is the primacy of the bass. Contrapuntally or coloristically, of course, it will have gained in importance, but at the expense of its role in defining the harmony. A beautiful example of this process already at work over a century ago is shown in the opening of Liszt's *Vallée d'Obermann,* where the melodic action of the bass clouds the harmony. Not until the return of the theme adds a new bass underneath the original one is the situation made clear. A further step in this direction is taken by Mahler, who by his polyphonically opposed chords points the way towards polytonality in the magical cowbell passage in the first movement of his Sixth Symphony. A more thoroughgoing example is Stravinsky's *Symphonies pour instruments à vent,* a more truly polytonal work than any of Milhaud's often-cited *Saudades,* which in fact present only extended and elaborated harmonies over a single real bass.

There are other forces at work undermining the primacy of the lowest voice. Impressionistic parallelism, which reduces its role to that of coloristic doubling, is too well known to require citation. Less frequent, but possibly more important in the light of later developments, is the masking of the true harmonic bass by a decorative voice below it, a technique seen clearly in the repetition of the opening of *La Fille aux cheveux de lin*. Another device, common to the Impressionists and Mahler, is the *ostinato*. From one point of view the persistent voice is emphasized, but at the same time it is removed from the sphere of action. In Debussy, as later in Stravinsky, the *ostinato* results in harmonic stasis; in Mahler there is a constant tension between the harmony implied by the motionless bass and those outlined by the moving voices and chords above it. In both cases the functional role of the bass is called into question.

So far no specific reference has been made to the problem of tonality. Except in comparatively rare cases, such as passages in *Le Sacre du printemps,* where an almost completely static tone or chord of reference is set up, tonality is created not by harmony alone, nor even by harmony and melody, but by their relationship with the rhythmic structure: in a word, by the phenomenon of the cadence. A discussion of certain rhythmic aspects, then, can no longer be postponed.

IV

Much of the vitality of the music of the Classical period derives from the constant interplay of meter and rhythm, the former determined by regular beats and measures and the latter by constantly varying motifs and phrases. This tension between the abstract and the concrete begins to break down during the 19th century, when phrase articulation is often either slavishly tied to the meter or else so completely liberated that the sense of the meter is almost lost. The retention of the measure in much Impressionistic music is purely conventional, and it is no wonder that later composers have abandoned the effort to keep an abstract pattern when it would conflict with the actual rhythm. For this reason the regularity of the meter in such composers as Webern must be carefully examined. Is it to be felt as a constantly present control? Is it a pure convention? Is it, as some would have us believe, an evidence of the composer's numerological superstitions?

The answers to such questions must always be given with specific reference to the text involved. When, as in the case of Example 11, the motif sets up a clear cross-rhythm, the explanation is relatively easy. Webern's Piano Variations, on the other hand, present the problem in an acute form. What has happened here, I think, is that the composer has called on a complex set of interrelationships of rhythmic, metric, dynamic, and textural factors to compensate for the tenuity of melodic and harmonic interest. In the first twelve measures of the last movement, for example, I find at least seven different time-divisions simultaneously functioning. These are set up by the meter (3/2), a possible cross-meter (5/4), the rhythm of the two-note motifs, the rhythm of the phrases, the tone-row, the dynamic alternations, and the linear pattern (Ex. 12).[2]

The really important question to ask in all such cases — and even in cases where the composer has deliberately tried to get rid of all traditional metrical measurement — is, can we locate the structural downbeat? If we can, then we can proceed with analytic concepts in some way analogous to those of the traditional rhythm and meter, phrase and cadence. If not, some completely new rhythmic theory must be devised. Some musicians, like Stockhausen, are trying to do this, but I have as yet seen no satisfactory one emerge.

By structural downbeat, of course, I do not mean the arbitrary accentuation of the first beat of every measure; I mean rather phenomena like the articulation by which the cadential chord of a phrase is identified, the weight by which the second phrase of a period is felt as resolving the first, the release of tension with which the tonic of a recapitula-

[2] Copyright 1937 by Universal Edition, A.G., Vienna. Reprinted by permission of Associated Music Publishers, Inc., sole agents for the United States.

Ex. 12

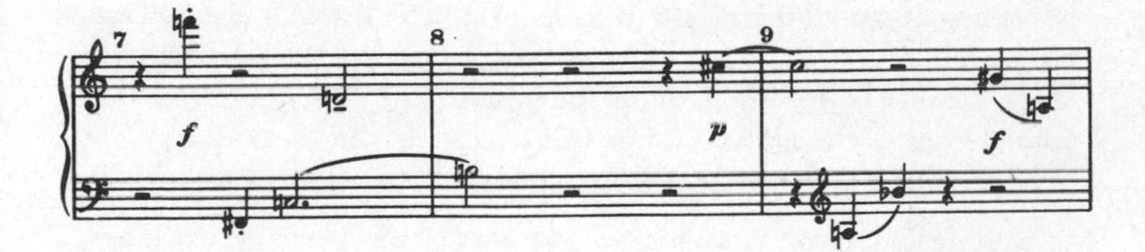

tion enters. (In the Webern example, I hear the downbeat as the E♭ at the beginning of measure 12; and I consider it no accident that it occurs at the beginning of a measure, preceded by a *ritardando.*)

It is just here that the importance of rhythm to the establishment of tonality emerges, for the cadence is the point in the phrase at which rhythmic emphasis and harmonic function coincide. It would be partly true to say that the cadence creates tonality, but it would be equally true to say that tonality creates the cadence. Where the cadence exists, it is impossible to hear music as completely atonal, even though one may be unable to define the key in conventional terms.

We know the signs by which a cadence can be recognized in traditionally tonal music: its position at the end of a phrase, the melodic resolution, the change of harmony. The actual downbeat may not always exactly coincide with the cadential point, but such unusual cases arise most often when the phrase is rhythmically prolonged (the feminine ending) or when it points ahead so clearly that the next phrase acts as a huge cadence to the first (as when an introductory section is followed by a main theme). In any case, keys are defined by the appearances of strong, cadential downbeats — whether clearly on the tonic as in most Classical examples, or on deceptive resolutions, as notably in the Prelude to *Tristan*.

The extent to which analogous principles govern the structure of contemporary music is surprising. A few examples will show them at work.

The opening of the second movement of Bartók's Fifth Quartet may prove puzzling until it is heard as an upbeat. The first downbeat comes on the D in measure 5, clinched by an even stronger cadence on the same tone (now supported by its fifth) in measure 10. The digression that follows suggests the key of C, but this tonality is not confirmed by the cadence, which, when it arrives in measure 20, is again clearly on D.

The first page of Sessions's Second Sonata for Piano is much less triadic; yet when the downbeat comes in measure 11, the harmony of B♭ is clearly established. Not only the V-I implied by the progression of fifths in the bass, but the melodic resolution to D, accented by the downward leap, points towards this tonal center, which is confirmed by what follows. In the second movement, no such clear downbeat is presented, but the two important feminine cadences of measures 177 and 190 both suggest an unstated resolution to E. The important downbeat of measure 191, coming as it then does on F, is in the nature of a neighboring harmony; and not until much later, at measure 213, does the expected E occur, its extension as a pedal for ten measures compensating for its long postponement. The last few measures of the Lento act as an upbeat released in the return of B♭ in the opening of the finale. But this in turn, after a long battle with conflicting elements, gives way at the last to the key of C, on which a downbeat is firmly established in the final chord.

Stravinsky is sometimes referred to as a "downbeat composer," by which I suppose is meant that he often emphasizes the beginnings rather than the endings of his phrases. This results in a weakening of the cadential sense, it is true, the phrases so accented being as it were huge feminine endings to their own opening chords. A typical example is the opening of the *Sérénade en la*. The harmonic progression would be described in traditional terms as VI^{6}_{3}-I^{5}_{3} in A minor; actually the F of the first chord is heard as hardly more than an appoggiatura resolving to the E of the second. This would appear to be no progression at all, in which case the phrase should be a huge *diminuendo.* Yet we cannot be too sure: in a similar situation at the beginning of the third movement of the *Symphony of Psalms,* the composer, by changing the mode and the orchestration at the cadential word *Dominum,* creates a clear accent even though the chord has remained essentially the same (C) throughout the phrase.

In any event, whatever we may decide about the reading of his phrase-accent in detail, Stravinsky is perfectly capable of producing a big structural downbeat at precisely the point where it is required. I need only point to the huge deceptive cadence that opens the Symphony in Three Movements, the dominant G of the introduction resolving finally upward to the A of the *ostinato* theme (rehearsal number 7); or to the way in which the Interlude acts as an upbeat to the C major of the finale.

More controversial is the attempt to find traces of tonal form in avowedly atonal compositions; yet I do not see how music like Schoenberg's, with its usually clear cadential structure, can fail to arouse certain traditional associations and responses. The previously cited *Klavierstück* Op. 33a begins with six chords, of which the second through the fifth are very easily—although not necessarily—heard as forming a progression referring to E minor. This in itself is nothing, but when the opening phrase is heard as an upbeat resolved in the third measure, and when the resolving sonority is recognized as a seventh on E, a tonal analogy is set up. The first section of the piece concludes even more unmistakably on E, with the added emphasis of a *ritardando;* and the theme that follows in measure 14 gives the effect of a sudden shift of key. In the recapitulation, the *ritardando* of measure 34 again calls attention to the following downbeat, where the E appears in the upper voice, but supported in the bass by A—in the manner of a deceptive cadence on IV. It remains for the final cadence to confirm the E, which is so strong that it is not dislodged by the dissonant tones with which it is here surrounded.

Several objections can be made to the above account: that it picks out isolated points without reference to the movement between them, that the "cadences" on E are a result of the fact that the row ends on that note, that such analysis is irrelevant to music in this style.

To the first count I plead guilty. I have indeed picked out isolated points, because these seemed to me to be the important "full-cadences" of the piece. (Important "half-cadences" occur at measures 9, 24, and 32.) The movement between them cannot, I grant, be explained in simple tonal terms. At some points, linear or contrapuntal motion dominates—in which case the melodic principles suggested above will indicate the logic of the chosen cadences. At other points the sonorities themselves dominate—and these can of course be shown as derived from the opening chords. As a result the entire piece can be heard as a development of its original cadential progression—that is, as analogous to a traditional structure.

I agree that the cadences are partially due to the use of the row. Depending on one's point of view, this effect is a virtue or a vice of Schoenberg's twelve-tone technique. It may even have been one of the points persuading him to turn towards the system, away from freer atonal methods. In no case can the argument invalidate the actual musical result.

To the charge of irrelevancy, I answer that one who cannot indeed hear such cadential phenomena in this music must judge the analysis to be prescriptive and inapplicable. But one who does hear them must admit to that extent the validity of the approach. He may counter that one ought not to hear the music in this way; but he is then criticizing the music, not the analytical method. Unwanted cadential effects would be as great a flaw in atonal music as the chance appearance of a human figure in a non-representational painting.

V

The last point suggests that there is a relation between analysis and criticism. It is not a simple one. Analysis can often reveal flaws in a work, it is true — often but not always. If it were dependable in this regard, we should be able to decide definitively between the disputed C♯ and C𝄪 in the last movement of Beethoven's Sonata Op. 109 (measure 55) or whether the famous A♮ in Schoenberg's Op. 33a is indeed an A♭ (measure 22). But unfortunately such cases all too often work both ways: the C𝄪 that from one point of view prepares for the advent of D two measures later might have been avoided in order not to anticipate it; by the same token, although the A♭ seems more logical in the row-structure (in spite of the A♮ lacking in the left-hand), it may somewhat spoil the freshness of the A♭-E♭ fifth that comes soon after. The ear must be the ultimate judge of such subtleties, but insofar as analysis trains and sharpens the ear it makes its contribution to the final decision.

It would be tempting to go further and state that analysis can demonstrate the quality of a work, but this requires a faith in rationality that I am unable to summon. Judgment of final excellence must be fundamentally intuitive. If analysis leads one to condemn a work he nevertheless continues to hear as good, he must conclude that there is something wrong either with his ear or with his method. Since he cannot dispense with the only pair of ears he has, upon whose evidence the examination should have been based in the first place, he must blame his method. He must then find a new one based on his own hearing, one that will substantiate, not contradict, his musical judgment. He may then claim that analysis has established the excellence of the work in question, but, he will be wrong; his own judgment will have established the analysis.

One positive point emerges here, and it is a crucial one. The good composition will always reveal, on close study, the methods of analysis needed for its own comprehension. This means that a good composition manifests its own structural principles, but it means more than that. In a wider context, it is an example of the proposition that a work of art ought to imply the standards by which it demands to be judged. Most criticism today tacitly accepts the truth of this statement and sets about discovering the standards implied by a given work and testing how well it lives up to them. For investigation of this kind, analysis is naturally of primary importance.

Criticism should take a further step, however, and the best criticism does. It should question the value of the standards. A work that sets no clear standard denies or defies the possibility of evaluation; one that does set its standard fails or succeeds insofar as it measures up to it; one that measures up completely is at least flawless — but its value cannot exceed the value of its own standard. It is this final step that is completely beyond the confines of analysis.

The music of Webern is a prominent case in point. No serious critic denies the perfection of his forms and the complete consistency of his style. Its paucity of normal melodic and harmonic interests has been mentioned above, but in connection with other values that, replacing these, uniquely characterize his manner. What is seldom questioned is the significance of the style itself — of the restrictive standard (for it is a restrictive one) that Webern set for his own music. Are the limits too narrow to permit accomplishment at the very highest level? Only a decision of this point can determine one's final evaluation of the composer. It is a decision that depends on one's beliefs about the limits and aims of art in general and is thus not exclusively musical, although it must at the same time be peculiarly musical. It must be made on faith, and it must be accepted or rejected in the same spirit.

SHOP TALK BY AN AMERICAN COMPOSER

By ELLIOTT CARTER

WHEN I agreed to discuss the rhythmic procedures I use in my music, I had forgotten, for the moment, the serious doubts I have about just such kinds of discussion when carried on by the composer himself. That a composer can write music that is thought to be of some interest is, of course, no guarantee that he can talk illuminatingly about it. It is especially hard for him to be articulate because inevitably his compositions are the result of innumerable choices — many unconscious, many conscious, some quickly made, others after long deliberation, all mostly forgotten when they have served their purpose. At some time or other, this sorting and combining of notes finally becomes a composition. By that time many of its conceptions and techniques have become almost a matter of habit for the composer and he is only dimly aware of the choices that first caused him to adopt them. Finally, in an effort to judge the work as an entity, as another might listen to it, he tries to forget his intentions and listen with fresh ears. What he is aiming at, after all, is a whole in which all the technical workings are interdependent and combine to produce the kind of artistic experience that gives a work its validity and in so doing makes all its procedures relevant. There is no short-cut to achieving this final artistic relevance. No technique is of much intrinsic value; its importance for the composer and his listeners lies only in the particular use made of it to further the artistic qualities and character of an actual work. If in discussing his works, therefore, he points out a procedure, he is bound to feel that he is drawing attention to something of secondary importance and by dwelling on it misleading others into thinking of it as primary. Schoenberg expressed such doubts in essays on his use of the twelve-tone method. And he was right, for certainly the twelve-tone aspect of his works accounts for only a part of their interest, perhaps not the most important part. For from Opus 25 to his last works the number of different kinds of compositions he wrote illustrates the very broad range of expression and conception and the wide variety of musical techniques that can incorporate the system and yet be distinguished from it.

In any discussion of specifically contemporary procedures, there are a few serious risks involved that must be constantly borne in mind. The first is the danger of rapid and wide dissemination of oversimplified formulas that shortens their life. It is obvious that one technical fad after another has swept over 20th-century music as the music of each of its leading composers has come to be intimately known. Each fad lasted a few years, only to be discarded by the succeeding generation of composers, then by the music profession, and finally by certain parts of the interested public. So that through over-use many of the striking features of the best works lost freshness, it was hard for those close to music to listen to these works for a time, and many of the better works disappeared from the repertory without a trace. Such a formula as the Impressionists' parallel ninth chords, for instance, wore itself out in the tedious arrangements of popular music current until recently. Each of the trends of our recent past — primitivism, machinism, neo-Classicism, *Gebrauchsmusik,* the styles of Bartók and Berg and now those of Schoenberg and Webern — has left and will leave in its trail numbers of really gifted composers whose music, skillful and effective as it is, is suffocated, at least for a time, by its similarity to other music of the same type. Of course, ultimately this faddishness is trivial, but its mercurial changes today have made the life of many a composer a great trial, more even than in the time of Rossini, who is now generally thought to have been one of the first outstanding composers to have given up composing because he could not change with the times.

The tendency to fad has been greatly encouraged by the promulgation of systems, particularly harmonic systems. Many recent composers following Schoenberg, Hindemith, and Messiaen have gained renown by circulating descriptions of their systems even in places where their music was not known. This kind of intellectual publicity can lead to a dead end even more quickly than the older fads derived from the actual sound of music in styles the composer did not even bother to explain.

The popularity of modern harmonic systems is, unfortunately, easy to understand. Textbooks led music students to think of harmony as a well-ordered routine, and when they found it to be less and less so in the years from Wagner to the present, they were much troubled — and still are — by the gap between what they learn and what they hear in modern music. For mature composers, lack of system is usually not much of a problem since they write, as they probably always have, what sounds right to them. This "rightness" has come, I suppose, from a developed sensitivity and experience that take time to acquire. When modern systems of harmony that were orderly and easy to explain appeared they filled an important pedagogical need for the inexperienced.

The very ease with which any of these systems can be used has its obvious dangers, as I have said. With the help of these and other shortcuts a vast amount of music is being written today, far more than can ever be played, than can ever be judged or widely known. At the same time there seems to be little corresponding development of discrimination, or even of ability or desire to listen to new music, little expansion of opportunities for performance, at least in this country. The struggle to be performed and to be recognized makes it very hard for one not to become, even against one's will, some kind of system-monger, particularly if one uses certain procedures that are considered effective. For among students there is today a hunger for new formulas, and they constitute an interested public.

Obviously the only way to withstand the disturbing prospect of being swept away by a change in fad is to plunge into the even more disturbing situation of trying to be an individual and finding one's own way, as most of us have tried to do, not bothering too much about what is or will be sanctioned at any given moment by the profession and the public. We may then have to lead our lives producing works "too soon" for their time as Webern did, if they are not really "too late" since, if professional, they presuppose an attentive public which seems to be getting rarer. We are caught in a development dictated by convictions impossible to change with the fads.

All this is to say that I do not consider my rhythmic procedures a trick or a formula. I do not even feel that they are an integral part of my musical personality, especially in the way I used them in my First String Quartet (1951), which delves elaborately into polyrhythms. As I have suggested, all aspects of a composition are closely bound together, and for this reason I cannot give an orderly exposition of any without bringing in a large perspective of ideas. So I do not know where to begin, and I need your help in directing this discussion to regions that will be interesting and useful to you. Almost anything I might say, I suppose, preferably on musical subjects, might be considered relevant to the subject you have so kindly invited me to discuss here.

Question: In the program notes of your Variations for Orchestra which you wrote for the Louisville performance, you described your method of variation as being a method of transformation, which you compared to the transformation from one life-stage to another of some marine animals. What did you mean by this?

Answer: As musicians you are all familiar with the problems of program notes. Technical discussions baffle the greater part of the audience and the few who do understand are apt to feel that the composer is a calculating monster, particularly since musical terms are ponderous, not always very definite in meaning, and too often give the impression of complexity when describing something very obvious to the ear. If I had described the augmentations, diminutions, retrograde inversions as they occur, this would have been positively bewildering to the public and would not have helped it to listen — certainly not the first time. So I tried to find a comparison that would help the listener to grasp my general approach. Serious music must appeal in different ways. Its main appeal, however, emerges from the quality of the musical material or ideas and perhaps even more from their use in significant continuities, but does not always depend on grasping the logic of the latter on first hearing. There has to be something left for the second time, if there ever is a second time.

As in all my works, I conceived this one as a large, unified musical action or gesture. In it, definition and contrast of character decrease during the first variations, arriving at a point of neutrality in the central variation, then increase again to the finale, which comprises many different speeds and characters. This work was thought of as a series of character studies in various states of interaction with each other both within each variation and between one and the next. Activity, development, type of emphasis, clearness or vagueness of definition, I hoped would also contribute to characterization. Form, rhythmic and development processes as well as texture and thematic material differ in each one for this reason.

The characteristic effort of the serious composer, as I see it, is not so much in the invention of musical ideas in themselves, as in the invention of interesting ideas that will also fill certain compositional requirements and allow for imaginative continuations. Serious music appeals to a longer span of attention and to a more highly developed auditory memory than do the more popular kinds of music. In making this appeal, it uses many contrasts, coherences, and contexts that give it a wide scope of expression, great emotional power and variety, direction, uniqueness, and a fascination of design with many shadings and qualities far beyond the range of popular or folk music. Every moment must count somehow, as must every detail. For a composer it is not always easy to find a passage that fits the particular situation and moment at which it appears in the composition, that carries to a further point some idea previously stated, that has the appropriate expressive quality motivated by what has been heard and yet is a passage that sounds fresh and alive.

As far as I am concerned, I am always interested in a composer's phrases and their shape and content, the way he joins them, the type of articulation he uses, as well as the general drift or continuity of a large section, and the construction of a whole work. The small details of harmony, rhythm, and texture fall naturally into place when one has interesting conceptions of these larger shapes.

Q: What do you mean by metric modulation?

A: If you listen to or look at any part of the first or last movement of my First String Quartet, you will find that there is a constant change of pulse. This is caused by an overlapping of speeds. Say, one part in triplets will enter against another part in quintuplets and the quintuplets will fade into the background and the triplets will establish a new speed that will become the springboard for another such operation. The structure of such speeds is correlated throughout the work and gives the impression of varying rates of flux and change of material and character, qualities I seek in my recent works. The wish to accomplish this in the domain of heavily emphasized contrapuntal contrasts led me to work out the plan of metric modulation described by Richard Goldman.[1]

Q: Why are the contrapuntal lines in your quartet so much alike, using equal note-values?

A: You cannot have listened to the work very carefully or looked at the score. Of the nine notes in the first four measures, there are seven different lengths, the longest 18 times the shortest. There are, it is true, a few places near the beginning in which several contrapuntal parts each of equal note-values are combined, but in complete polyrhythmic contrast emphasized by intervallic, bowing, and expressive

[1] Richard Goldman, *The Music of Elliott Carter,* in *The Musical Quarterly,* XLIII (1957), 151.

contrasts. In these I was particularly anxious to present to the listener the idea of polyrhythmic textures in its most definite form, for even this quality of texture develops during the work, leading, in the second movement, to a four-part fragmented canon in continuous sixteenths and, in later movements, to lines of much notational irregularity. But even if the values were more frequently equal than they are, as for instance in the polyrhythmic, posthumous Études of Chopin, I cannot see that this would be a real objection, as you imply. Many a fine work has dealt in continuous streams of equal note-values.

Q: Does your music have any harmonic plan?

A: A chord, a vertical group of pitches either simultaneously sounded or arpeggiated, like a motif, is a combination to be more or less clearly remembered and related to previous and future chords heard in the same work. Whether the composer is conscious of it or not, a field of operation with its principles of motion and of interaction is stated or suggested at the beginning of any work. The field may be tonal, employ traditional harmony, or it may be unrelated to traditional harmony, as my music seems to be nowadays, in which case I feel it imperative to establish clearly, near the beginning, the principles upon which the composition moves. Once this field of operation is established, its possibilities are explored, interesting new aspects of it are revealed, patterns of action of contrasting types emerge as the work goes along. A work whose world is not clearly defined loses a great deal of possible power and interest, one whose world is too narrow and restricted runs the risk of being thin, although if the world is unusual enough this narrowness can produce a kind of hallucinatory quality — one that I do not concern myself with in my own works. This extension of the traditional methods of coherence can rarely be attained nowadays solely by intuition, I think, because of the vast number of musical means, new and old, that we know. Some composers, it is true, insulate themselves from new musical experiences in an effort not to be distracted. Others, whose curiosity and interest prompt them to follow what is going on, feeling, perhaps, as Charles Ives did, that "eclecticism is part of his duty — sorting potatoes means a better crop next year,"[2] have to make a number of conscious choices and establish the frame in which to work before they can compose at all.

In my First String Quartet, I did use a "key" four-note chord, one of the two four-note groups, that joins all the two-note intervals

[2] Charles Ives, *Essays Before a Sonata,* New York, 1920, p. 94.

into pairs, thus allowing for the total range of interval qualities that still can be referred back to a basic chord-sound. This chord is not used at every moment in the work but occurs frequently enough, especially in important places, to function, I hope, as a formative factor. It is presented in various kinds of part-writing and interval combination, the number of notes is increased and diminished in it, in ways familiar to all of you. The chord, here in its closest position, showing its content of intervals of a diminished fifth and less, is also used both in many intervallic inversions and in total inversion:

Ex. 1

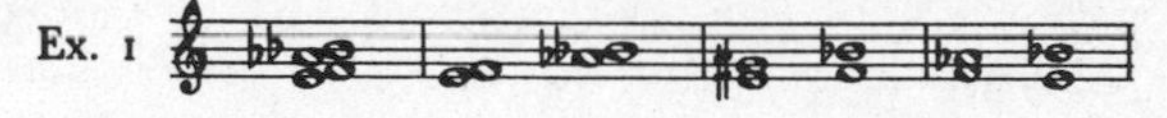

Here is an example of its use in counterpoint that occurs in measure 477 of the last movement, where the quality of the chord is strongly dwelt on—each vertical combination except the last being made up of it:

Ex. 2

Q: Did you try to shape the free writing found in your quartet into formal patterns?

A: Since I consider form an integral part of serious music, I certainly did. Strange as it may seem, the intention of composing a work that depended so much on change of movement and polyrhythmic texture involved me not only in special questions of clarity and audibility that one does not usually have to face, but in special problems of form also. One of the solutions I tried, to keep this rather free-sounding technique from seeming haphazard and thus lose its connection with the progress of the work and the attentive listener's ear, was to establish thematic patterns made up of components of different ideas that could be separated. This feature emerges in the last movement, many of whose motifs are disintegrated to produce polyrhythms (Ex. 3). This is only one of the many ways I tried, hoping to give the impression of that combination of freedom and control that I greatly admire in many works of art.

Ex. 3

Q: Do you use the twelve-tone system?

A: Some critics have said that I do, but since I have never analyzed my works from this point of view, I cannot say. I assume that if I am not conscious of it, I do not. Naturally out of interest and out of professional responsibility I have studied the important works of the type and admire many of them a great deal. I have found that it is apparently inapplicable to what I am trying to do, and is more of a hindrance than a help. Its nature is often misunderstood, it is a building material and not the building, and it allows, I think, for certain greater freedoms than were possible using traditional harmony with its very strict rules of part-writing, just as reinforced concrete allows for certain construction patterns impossible with stone. I must also say that having known many of these works all of my adult life, I hope the recent fad will not cause them to seem commonplace too soon. The results of total serialization are more recalcitrant to musical handling, I think.

Q: Do you mean to say that your rhythmic method is not a product of serialization?

A: It is not. But it is true that like all music, mine goes from one thing to another—the pattern on which serialization is based, but my choices of where to start and where to go are controlled by a general plan of action that directs both the continuity and the expression. Single details, chords, rhythmic patterns, motifs, textures, registers follow each other in a way that combines them into clearly perceivable larger patterns and then patterns of these patterns, and to me this cannot be easily accomplished with total serialization, at least the kind I study my way through in European articles these days. Perhaps another more useful and not so arbitrary kind of serialization could be devised. The present one resembles the turning of a kaleidoscope and usually produces not much more—or less—interesting results. Indeed it can be fascinating to listen to the total repertory of pitches, note-values, timbres, registers, and dynamics being touched upon in rapid succession and from a point of view we are unaccustomed to. But the cumulative effect of this is self-defeating since neither the attention nor the memory is appealed to. For who can decipher, by ear, the complexities of total serialization in most works of the sort? On the other hand, those in which this process can be followed are too obvious to be of any interest.

Q: What is your attitude about performance difficulty?

A: I realize with brutal clarity that orchestral music requiring a lot of rehearsal can, by the nature of American musical life, find very few, if any, performances. This is not true of difficult music for soloists or small standardized instrumental groups, for obvious reasons. Our orchestral musicians are trained to play in the demanding scores of Strauss, Mahler, Debussy, Ravel, and early Stravinsky. One might imagine that one of the obligations of a present-day composer would be to use the skills of these excellently trained musicians to their full, lest their abilities deteriorate for want of use; that the challenge of good, effective yet technically advanced scores would be helpful in maintaining high performance standards in an orchestra, if not in raising them, as it did in the past. But this does not seem to be a consideration here, and, as you and I know, new works that make an immediate effect with a minimum of effort and time are favored. The real effort goes into the standard repertory, where it is more widely appreciated. Therefore, a composer who wishes to write orchestral music and get it played here has to tailor his work to these practical conditions, whether his ideas are suitable to such exploitation or not. Those who find that they can do nothing of interest under these conditions either give up writing orchestral music or, if they cannot, hope for European performances of their works. For these reasons, the scores of our composers often show a lack of practical experience that reveals itself in conventionality and timidity. How can a man be adventurous, under the circumstances that obtain here? Any casual look at the European scores written since the war will show how far in advance of us even beginners are there in this respect. As in many other things, we may be willing to accept the final, accomplished results of European training and experimental efforts but we cannot afford and are impatient with the step-by-step experience needed to produce them.

Naturally, music that is both difficult and yet practical to play is not easy to write, and it may even be difficult to listen to. It does not make for a comfortable life to have this as one's mode of expression. There is an undoubted beauty in reducing things to their essentials or to their simplest form if something is gained thereby. When a composer cannot find an interesting and satisfying way of writing easy music, he is at least free, here, to use the level of difficulty he needs to set forth his ideas completely—even if this results in no performances. But I see no reason for being just difficult. Whenever difficult passages seem imperative in my works, I try to make them especially rewarding once they are played correctly.

For I regard my scores as scenarios, auditory scenarios, for performers to act out with their instruments, dramatizing the players as individuals and participants in the ensemble. To me the special teamwork of ensemble playing is very wonderful and moving, and this feeling is always an important expressive consideration in my chamber music.

Q: Have you ever thought of composing electronic music?

A: Naturally, I have often been intrigued with the idea of electronic music and have visited the Milan electronic studio several times to find out what is being done. I must say that almost all I have heard seems to me to be in a primary stage, and has not resolved some fundamental problems of matching and comparison of sounds that would raise it above the physical scariness that makes this music useful for television science fiction and horror programs. As far as composing it myself is concerned, you can imagine that since I am very enmeshed in the human aspect of musical performance, I would find it hard to think in terms of the impersonal sound patterns of electronic music. Certainly, impatience at not being able to hear my works in performance and impatience at the inaccuracies of some performances have occasionally made me wish that I could have a machine that would perform my music correctly and without all the trouble and possible disappointments associated with live performances.

Q: What do you think of Charles Ives now?

A: My opinions about Charles Ives as a composer have changed many times since I first came to know him during my high-school years in 1924-25, but my admiration for him as a man never has. No one who knew him can ever forget his remarkable enthusiasm, his wit, his serious concern and love for music, and his many truly noble qualities which one came to notice gradually because they appeared casually, without a trace of pompousness, pretention, or "showing off." Attracted to him by a youthful enthusiasm for contemporary music, I first admired, and still do, the few advanced scores privately available in those days, the *Concord Sonata,* the *Three Places in New England,* and some of the *114 Songs.* However, after I had completed strict musical studies here and abroad, I saw these works in a different light. Misgivings arose which I expressed with considerable regret in several articles in *Modern Music* after the first performance of the *Concord Sonata* in New York in 1939. My doubts were of two kinds. First, there seemed to be very large amounts of undifferentiated confusion, especially in the orchestral works, during which many conflicting things happen at once without apparent concern either for the total effect or for the distinguishability of various levels. Yet in each score such as the *Robert Browning Overture,* the *Fourth of July,* and the second and fourth movements of the Fourth Symphony where this confusion is most frequent, it is the more puzzling because side by side with it is a number of passages of great beauty and originality. Even more disturbing to me then was his frequent reliance on musical quotations for their literary effect. In spite of these doubts, I continued for many years to help bring Ives's music before the public since he would do nothing for himself, rescuing, among other things, *The Unanswered Question* and *Central Park in the Dark* from the photostat volumes of his work he had left with the American Music Center. I arranged for first performances of these at a Ditson Fund Concert at Columbia University in, I think, 1949.

What interests me now is his vigorous presentation in music and essays of the conflict between the composer with vision and original ideas, the musical profession, and the American public. It is the living out of this conflict, made poignant by his strong convictions, the anger it produced, the various actions and attitudes it led him to, the retreat into a subjective world, and, unfortunately, the terrible toll of energy and health it took, that makes of Ives an artist really characteristic of America, not unlike Melville. Without the dimension of this struggle and the quality it gave his scores, his *Emersons* and *Hallowe'ens* would be of superficial and transitory interest.

His rage, which explodes between the waves of his transcendental visions in prose as it does in the scribbled comments in the margin of his musical manuscripts, reveals troubled concern over the problems of the American composer and his relations with the public. The music profession is castigated in one place as being more hide-bound, more materialistic, petty, bigotted, and unprincipled than the business world. The latter, his refuge from the bleak, meager life of the conventional American musician of his time, he respected and identified himself with enough to adopt an American business man's view of the artistic profession, one that was especially characteristic of that time of wealthy art-collectors. Making of the artist an anti-business man, Ives saw him as a prophet living in the pure, transcendent world of the spirit, above the mundane matters of money, practicality, and artistic experience. The 19th-century American dream of art and high culture, which Henry James liked to project against the sordid European background from which it came, was the source, as Aaron Copland and Wilfrid Mellers have pointed out, of Ives's greatest misfortune. In gradually retiring into this dream, he cut himself off from music's reality. Too many of his scores, consequently, were never brought to the precision of presentation and scoring necessary to be completely communicative to the listener —or so it seems now. One could say that Ives was unable completely to digest his experience as an American and make it into a unified and meaningful musical expression. The effort of remodelling the musical vocabulary to meet his own personal vision, almost without encouragement or help, was too great, and too often he had to let hymn tunes and patriotic songs stand for his experience without comment.

As I have said, Ives's life vividly presents the special conflicts inherent in the American composer's situation. Today, even more than in his time, the division between the musician's professional code of ethics, his traditional standards of skill and imagination established at another time in another place, and the present standards of behavior respected, sanctioned, and rewarded by the society that surrounds us, is very pronounced. The familiar training of a composer giving him knowledge and skill in the accumulation of musical techniques, past and present, and the development of skill in notating them, presupposes trained copyists and performers who can grasp what he means and respect his notations. It also presupposes critics and, if not a large public, at least an influential élite that will be able to perceive the sense of the composer's efforts and skill, value them and enable him to develop them further, by giving them careful consideration. When one or more of the links in this chain is not sufficiently developed or non-existent, as is often the case here today, the composer has a bitter fight just to keep his skill, let alone develop it.

This misfortune can be laid to the general lack of unanimity about and concern for the profession of composing on the part of the mass musical public that plays such an influential financial role in America. By training, the composer learns to write for a musically educated public that is also an influential élite, which does not exist and may never exist here. He cannot help but feel that he will be heard by a large majority of listeners and even performers that disagree with him, if they have any opinions at all, on the most fundamental issues of his art. Questions of style, system, consonance, dissonance, themes, non-themes, being original or an imitator, which imply some agreement on fundamentals, are not the stumbling blocks. A professional composer has today, as Ives certainly had, the training to be "communicative," "melodious," "expressive," qualities considered to have a wide appeal, just as he is now trained to use advanced techniques that will be appreciated by only a few professionals. How shall he decide? He is free, here, to do what he likes, of course, but it does not take him long to realize that whatever he chooses to do, radical or conservative, his music will further divide into small sub-groups the handful of people who will listen to contemporary music at all. Not one of these small sub-groups has the power or the interest to convince the large public by publicity or other means of the validity of its opinions, as happens in the other arts here. While diversity of opinion is much to be welcomed, where so little support exists such decimation of interest, one hesitates regretfully to conclude, can lead to cancelling of efforts and ultimately to their negation.

Even America's panacea, publicity, seems strangely useless in this field. Good reviews do not, often, lead to further performances, but they do help to sell more recordings. One might have thought that Ives, now so much discussed and publicly admired, would be often heard. That a number of his recordings have been discontinued, that only a few of his easiest pieces are heard while some of his more remarkable works are still unplayed or scarcely known, is surely an indication of how confused and desperate is the relation between the composer, the profession, publicity, and the musical public.

NOTES ON
A PIECE FOR TAPE RECORDER

By VLADIMIR USSACHEVSKY

Choosing the Sound Material

A DISCUSSION of electronic music inevitably brings up the important question of how the availability of new sound materials and the direct participation of a composer in shaping these materials may tend to influence his methods of composition. Any experienced composer knows the sounds and capabilities of the instruments he is going to use in his score. In the tape medium — my readers will remember that this includes sounds produced non-electronically and stored on tape, as well as sounds electronically produced — and especially in the category of non-electronic sounds, a sound is often chosen not for what it is but rather for what it will become through electronic modification.

I believe that the virtually unlimited source of sounds available to a composer who works with tape requires perhaps as great vigilance in selecting the proper material as would normally be exercised in determining an orchestral palette, if not greater. It is tempting to parade unusual sounds; and the structural unity of a composition can be seriously weakened by diverting attention with an overabundance of such sounds. To avoid creating these distractions in *A Piece for Tape Recorder,* I restricted my raw material to the following:

Non-electronic: a gong, a piano, a single stroke on a cymbal, a single note on a kettledrum, the noise of a jet plane, a few chords on an organ.

Electronic: four pure tones, produced on an oscillator, a tremolo produced by the stabilized reverberation of a click from a switch on a tape recorder.

The sounds of the piano and of the jet noise are used in an episodic manner, and serve to impart dynamic punctuation to otherwise slowly evolving sound texture. The remaining sounds are used in a secondary role of background accompaniment, sometimes obviously as plain old-fashioned sustained tones, sometimes with more subtle variations of timbre. The over-all structure seeks to effect a gradual transition from a type of sound material that possessed a certain clearly recognizable musical quality to the type of sound that is more closely identified with a complex noise spectrum. It was my hope that this transition would appear natural, and that the sense of unity could be preserved through a motivic affinity.

All of these sounds were drawn from the library of sound on tape maintained at the Columbia University Studio. Two of the non-electronic sounds were already used once in my earlier piece, *Sonic Contours*. Other material existed as the result of the extensive experimentation by Otto Luening and myself which preceded making our score for Orson Welles's production of *King Lear*.

Notation

The composition was put together from sketches that represented durations, timbres, and dynamics on a four-line chart. This chart was used when synchronizing the four tape recorders in the final mixing of the four tapes on which the entire sound material was prepared. The pitches were given approximate notation in a separate sketch made on regular music paper.

Since the Copyright Office in Washington does not grant a copyright on a work as a musical composition unless it is written or printed in ordinary musical notation, I rather unwillingly spent forty hours to produce a score, one page of which is reproduced here. My reluctance was based on the impossibility of describing many of the sounds in conventional musical notation. I thus attempted a pitch-approximation of the sounds, at the same time placing them exactly where they occur on the time scale. The following explanation of the methods used to represent durations, pitch, and dynamics accompanied the score.[1]

Durations

This score represents a musical transcription of sounds on four tracks of magnetic tape (each indicated by a Roman numeral) used in the final mixing

[1] The example and the explanation are copyright 1956 by Vladimir Ussachevsky. The work was completed in April of that year and has been recorded by Composers Recordings, Inc. on their disc CRI-112.

to obtain the composition. In this respect it is similar to a conventional four-line score; however, the difference lies in the flexible interpretation of conventional symbols resulting from calculating durations in terms of seconds, the expedient necessitated by characteristic flexibility of time units in individual lines. Frequently, therefore, an entire phrase is clocked with a stop-watch and notated as accurately

as possible within the proper time-space, without an attempt to establish precisely the relative value of each note to an over-all common denominator. Throughout the piece the latter, however, is roughly one whole note for one second. In some cases where the length of sound exceeds 20 seconds, the beginning of it is indicated by and the end by . The absence of the above or any other symbol indicates silence.

Pitch

Many sounds used in this score are rich in harmonics, and the pitches indicated are frequently only of the predominant pitch impression. This latter, however, is indicated in the proper range as accurately as possible, and, on the whole, with a far closer pitch approximation than is customarily used in describing gong, cymbal, and drum pitches in the percussion part of an orchestral score.

Dynamics

A decibel scale of dynamics is used in addition to the usual musical dynamic marks to indicate intensity accurately. The arabic numerals throughout the score refer to the number of seconds from the beginning, and each measure, suggested by the small, regular dividing marks, is calculated in terms of one-second duration. Thus all the entrances and cessations of sounds are very precisely indicated.

Letter Symbols Describing the Sounds

Each component of a descriptive symbol is set apart by a semicolon; the letter or group of letters preceding a semicolon refers to the origin or character of a sound, the letter or two hyphenated letters following the semicolon describe the manner of bringing the sound into being. The third letter describes additional modification of sounds.

Reverberated	R
Metallic, soft-struck	M; s-s
Metallic, hard-struck	M; h-s
Percussion	pr.
Electronic sound	El.
Electronic tone-cluster	Etn clst
Electronic treatment	el
Piano	P
Middle of a note	><
Roll and tremolo	∿∿∿∿∿
Oscillator	Osc.
Organ	O.
Wind	W. ∿∿∿∿∿

Developing the Sound Material

Without describing in detail the technical processes,[2] I hope it is understood that the available means of manipulating recorded sounds make it almost mandatory for a composer to run through a certain number of routine experiments before he can determine the full range of his raw material. Experience gradually teaches one what to expect. I now habitually imagine a sound as if it were changed by the following mutation techniques, among others:

pitch transposition through variation of tape speed;
snipping off the attack and listening to the body of the sound itself;

[2] Interested readers are referred to my article, *Processes of Experimental Music,* in *Audio-Engineering Society Journal,* Vol. 6, No. 3, July 1958, pp. 202-08.

playing it backwards;
depriving it of some of its harmonics through filtering;
reverberating it.

An intricate interrelation exists between an abstract formal concept which a composer might have formed about his forthcoming composition and the manner of developing his raw sound material. There can be a decided interaction between the two which makes itself felt through all the early experimental stages. In my *Piece for Tape Recorder* such interaction entailed a certain give and take between the initially vague formal plans and the composing of sound patterns from single sounds. I proposed to utilize the timbre of a gong, stretched to span almost the entire audible range, as a unifying element— a kind of a timbre leitmotif, if you will. But there are many more than thirteen ways of sounding a gong and coaxing a maximum of variety from its rich content.

For example, while melodic use of large gongs is impractical for the conventional orchestra (a series of small groups of Javanese gongs can be used, but their pitch succession will vary from one set to another), in the tape medium, creation of any type of scale is possible from any type of sound.

Since an appreciable change in timbre takes place during the life of the sound of a gong, I sampled various portions of it. The moment of striking the surface with a mallet contains several noise components which quickly disappear. Within a few seconds much of the metallic quality is gone, but the timbre is still complex. By first cutting the attack and then sampling various portions of the remaining sound, I arrived at three basic variations of the timbres. The middle of the gong sound, somewhat pale but tremulous, was made by transposition into a melodic line consisting of seven pitches of even duration which span a range of an octave and a half (see the example, Track II, between the 47- and 70-second marks). The sound containing the attack was used in two different ways. In one, it was modified by slurring the attack through speed variation and by electronic reverberation creating a succession of four pitches which rise chromatically and die out (see Track I, between the 58- and 82-second marks). In the other, the full impact of the attack was preserved. A thunder of six evenly spaced strokes of this sound was arranged in an ascending pattern at the interval of a fourth, to serve as a strong *sforzando* punctuation. (This occurs approximately 99 seconds after the opening of the piece.) The same sound, with the attack preserved, was further transposed over many octaves to a high register, where the resulting pinched, ping-like quality of the compressed attack easily penetrated through a broad, wind-like spectrum. This sound was used frequently in the second half of the composition. Finally, a dynamically shaped, sustained line was derived from a long resonance of a large gong played backwards. In this instance the attack was faded out and a long, impressive, and relatively smooth crescendo was obtained. This sound was quite useful as a subtly changing lower and inner sustained tone (see Tracks II and III, up to the 42-second mark).

As I have pointed out, it was my intention to create a certain feeling of unity by developing much of the material from a single kind of timbre. As it turned out, all other sound material became secondary in both thematic and timbral importance. In the category of instrumental sounds, a few patterns originating from the piano were subjected to only the simplest of transformations, without cutting of tape or dynamic shaping of any sort. A piano chord which is reverberated and played backwards supplies a brief *ostinato* at the opening of the work; later, clearly pianistic patterns, their pitch and speed doubled by an upward octave transposition, are heard four times. Still later, a long, organ-like pedal point, derived from a low piano tone with the attack cut off, is used.

A single note on a kettledrum served as the basis for the complex wind-like sound mentioned above. This sound, one of the oldest in our sound library at Columbia, had been previously used to construct several tape solo passages in *Rhapsodic Variations for Tape Recorder and Orchestra* and in *King Lear,* both written by Otto Luening and myself. In *A Piece for Tape Recorder,* its transpositions by tape-speed variation form a vertical sonority roughly akin to a minor seventh chord, which is in turn shifted up and down as a unit, its broad spectrum imparting a decidedly confused impression as far as pitch is concerned. More easily definable in its approximation of a pitch area is a sound of a cymbal which is used to form a brief three- to four-note motif appearing towards the end of the composition. The upper edge of the complex sound derived from this non-melodic instrument draws, as it descends, an easily perceived contour. Material derived from an organ is used very briefly in the form of two chords: once as a dynamic accent in a loud passage, and later as purely a timbre of a dark color. I employed electronically generated sounds sparingly. In a curious way they serve a tonally stabilizing function in the midst of complex sonorities which undulate between relative clarity and almost noise-like indefiniteness. A cluster of sinusoidal tones, with their characteristic "steady-state" quality unadulterated by reverberation, first appears in the 73rd second of the composition. Contrasted to this "dead-level" tone, a melodic line is constructed from an electronic warble-like tone, characterized by an intense vibrato, the rate of which is changed with every new pitch level. This helps take away the usual monotony, not to say irritation, often engendered by an electronically induced vibrato.

Formal Organization

Some composers do all the organization in the silence of the mind; others need the physical impact of the sound. Most composers indulge in some improvisation and retain, or attempt later to recapture, that part of their subconscious utterance which they feel belongs to their conception.

The tape medium is particularly felicitous for giving the composer a chance to hear and to shape his sound material as he proceeds. His decisions regarding the final form of a composition are not infrequently influenced by the results of his experimentation with the sound material. Nevertheless, some electronic composers maintain that an advantage of electronic music is that it can be completely realized by precise specification of certain acoustical and musical components. Others disdain the rigors of numerical "total organization" and let the sine tones fall where they may. Both sides have representatives who do not wish to have their compositions assume any one final form and prefer the sequences of patterns to be rearranged for each individual performance.[3]

It is outside of my topic to debate the comparative merits of these approaches. However, one must note the existence of the improvisatory element. Within the limits of my experience, I can testify that engaging in an experiment in which the machines themselves assist the improvisation is often valuable as a stimulant. Such improvisation can create sound patterns that would indeed be hard to imagine in advance. The improvisation also has the advantage of being recorded and, hence, available for examination. The value of improvisatory material ranges from zero upward, but there is no denying that it assists the composer's imagination in making decisions regarding sound materials and the evolution of a final form. This, to me, seems legitimate.

It must be made clear that the experimental procedure just described refers to using the machines to produce the mechanical repetition of single notes or patterns. Similarly, they can create modifications of

[3] This may raise some lively issues with the Office of Copyright which, one supposes, issues the birth certificates on the assumption that the composer's new baby will retain its features.

pitch relationships or timbre which can be induced either automatically by the machines themselves or by the continuous control of the operator. Skill of the subtlety approaching that of a performer is required to exercise such control. Creative experience is equally important for making those instant judgments which can directly influence the ultimate quality of the improvised material.

As I have said earlier, the interrelation between the development of the material and the final form of the work certainly played a part in the composition of *A Piece for Tape Recorder*. The abstract aim was two-fold. First of all, I wanted to achieve a kind of large, assymetrical arch on both a dynamic and a pitch scale. The ascent was to be accomplished through a series of little arches, while the descent would consist of a long, gently undulating line of a predominantly gray timbre, punctuated by fragments of the thematic material used in the first part. The second aim was to start the composition with a sound pattern possessing in large measure those qualities which would permit the listener to make associations with definite pitches and, at times, conventional rhythmic patterns. Gradually the timbres with a greater noise content would be introduced, but the motivic unity would persist. The composition was to end quietly with an impression that the last few notes were largely noise descending by discernible intervals of thirds, fourths, and sixths.

This plan was carried out in the finished work, and it seems that one reason for its thoughtful reception can be found in its sense of direction and unity. Dynamic punctuation, originating from diversified sound material, helps to separate main sections of the work. Unity is imparted by the motivic consistency and the derivation of the principle motif from one timbre, highly modified though it was by manipulations peculiar to the process of composition in electronic music.

EXTENTS AND LIMITS OF SERIAL TECHNIQUES

By ERNST KRENEK

The Title

THE propensity of present musical theory for terminology originally belonging to mathematics and physics is characteristic of a style of thinking essentially different from earlier ways of viewing the subject matter. Although some of this language sounds merely pretentious, it has nevertheless added useful terms to musical discussion. One of these is the concept of "parameter." It was introduced into recent music theory by Dr. Meyer-Eppler, of the Institute of Communication Theory at the University of Bonn, who was associated with the work of the electronic laboratory of the West German Radio at Cologne. It is borrowed from mathematics, where it means "a variable entering into the mathematical form of any distribution such that the possible values of the variable correspond to different distributions."[1]

Serial organization of a certain number of parameters of a musical process causes a certain number of other parameters to be left uncontrolled. A detailed study of the relationships of these two areas was the purpose of the seminar. The title did not, as was surmised by some, hint at a discrimination between accomplishments and shortcomings of serial thinking.

Definition

Serial music was defined as a method of composition that has been developed as a sequel of the twelve-tone technique inaugurated by Arnold Schoenberg around 1923. While the serial concept in that technique was embodied in the twelve-tone series, i.e. an ordering of the pitches to be adhered to throughout the course of the composition, the new idea of

[1] *American College Dictionary*, New York, 1948, p. 879.

serialism encompasses all aspects (or "parameters") of the musical process, such as timbre, dynamics, articulation, and above all, time, i.e. duration of the individual sounding elements and their mutual relationships in time, subordinating all these aspects to premeditated serial statements. In this view the twelve-tone technique appears to be a special, or limiting, case of serial music, similar to an interpretation of Newtonian mechanics as a limiting expression of the Special Theory of Relativity, which in turn has been explained as a limiting expression of that General Theory.

Method

Anton Webern and Olivier Messiaen were mentioned as the best-known generators of the new way of serial thinking, the former because of the extraordinary impact his work has exercised during the last twenty years or so, the latter above all through his experiments with "rhythmic rows" (or "modes") and his immediate influence on such composers as Boulez and Stockhausen. The discussion then turned to the significance and consequence of the gradual expansion of the musical area that was subjected to premeditated organization. It was recognized that serial ordering of the factor of time (i.e. premeditated fixation of points of entrance and duration of the individual musical elements) caused fundamental changes in the structure, appearance, perceptibility, and meaning of music. Therefore the larger part of the investigation was devoted to the methods of organizing serially the parameter of time. The discourse was mainly based on my own work in the serial style because my intimate knowledge of this work allowed succinct presentation of the relevant details, whereas the few available analyses of other composers' serial works are frequently ambiguous and far from enlightening.

The Principle of "Rotation"

By rotation we understand a procedure in which the elements of a given series systematically and progressively change their relative positions according to a plan which in itself is serially conceived in that the changes occur in regular phases.[2]

I applied this principle for the first time in a large choral work,

[2] In his book, *Die Komposition mit zwölf Tönen,* Berlin, 1952, p. 113 ff. and *passim,* Josef Rufer points out that Arnold Schoenberg occasionally let neighboring tones of his rows exchange places, or groups of tones change their positions within the row. Rufer's discourse and the examples quoted show that this was done sporadically and mainly in order to create a musical context that would not have been served as well by adhering to the premeditated succession of pitches.

Lamentatio Jeremiae Prophetae,[3] written in 1940 and 1941. The twelve-tone series of this work reads thus:

Ex. 1

Each of its two constituent six-tone groups is progressively modified by making the first tone the last:

Ex. 2

The patterns thus obtained may be called "diatonic" since they contain the same six tones. The roster of patterns is doubled by transposing all those of the left column of Ex. 2 to begin on F, all those of the right column to begin on B.

Ex. 3

[3] Bärenreiter-Verlag, Kassel.

These new patterns are "chromatic" because they eventually include all twelve tones. The rotation taking place was inspired by the construction of the Greek modal scales and their transposition into one "characteristic" octave. The purpose of the operation was not so much to make the serial design stricter, but rather to relax it, insofar as the wide variety of available six-tone patterns made it possible to remain within the frame of reference of the twelve-tone serial technique without constantly having to use complete twelve-tone rows. Thus it became possible to give various areas of the composition distinctive harmonic flavors. At that time no attempt was made to organize serially the selection and succession of the rotational patterns.

A more consistent and systematic application of the principle of rotation may be found in my orchestral work, *Circle, Chain and Mirror,*[4] written in 1956 and 1957 for the Basel Kammerorchester. The tone-row of this work reads as follows:

In the course of the composition twenty-four derivative forms of this row are employed. The principle of derivation may easily be apprehended by comparing the original row with its first three derivative forms (the tones in their original succession are numbered from 1 to 12):

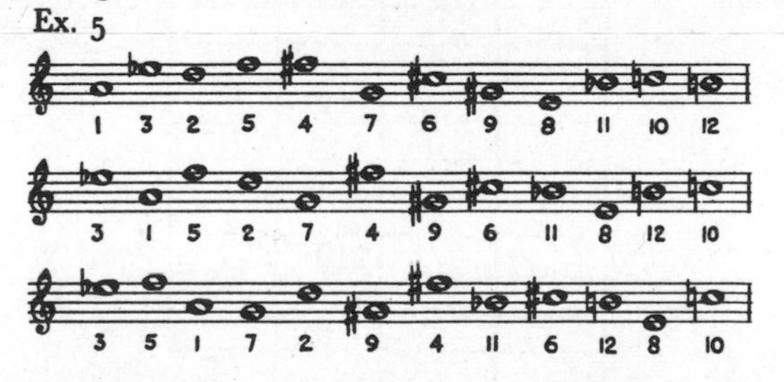

The rotation taking place here consists in forming a retrograde succession of each pair of two adjacent tones. After eleven such operations one arrives at the complete retrograde form of the original statement. The twelve following derivates represent the retrograde forms of the first twelve, and the twenty-fifth transformation is identical with the original. The same procedure was applied to the inverted form of the original series (see Ex. 6). This arrangement suggested the "circle" part of the title of the work.

[4] Original German title: *Kette, Kreis und Spiegel.* Bärenreiter-Verlag, Kassel.

The sequence in which the forty-eight rows thus obtained were used in the work was determined by the decision to have each original form followed by the second of the two forms of the inversion which would have for their first tones the last tone of the preceding original, while this inversion in turn would be followed by an original form beginning with the last tone of the preceding inversion. This interlocking arrangement is meant by the term "chain" in the title. The sequence of rows obtained through this operation may be partially seen in the following table (O=original, I=inversion, R=retrograde, RI=retrograde inversion):

O	I	R	RI
1			
	8		
6			
			12
10			
			4
4			
			10
12			
			6
		8	
			2
	1		
8			
	6		
		12	
	10		
		4	
	4		
		10	
	12		
		6	
			8
		2	
2			
	7		
5			
			11
9			
			3
3			

etc.

The symmetry resulting from this organization is obvious: The sequence 1, 6, 10, 4, 12 in lines 1 to 9 of the O column is identical with the sequence 1, 6, 10, 4, 12 in lines 13 to 21 of the I column. The same relation obtains as regards the sequences 12, 4, 10, 6, 2 in lines 4 to 12 of RI and 16 to 24 of R. The positions of I8 between O1 and 6 and of O8 between I1 and 6 are equally symmetrical and correspond to the positions of the 8s in R and RI between 2 and 6 of RI and R respectively.

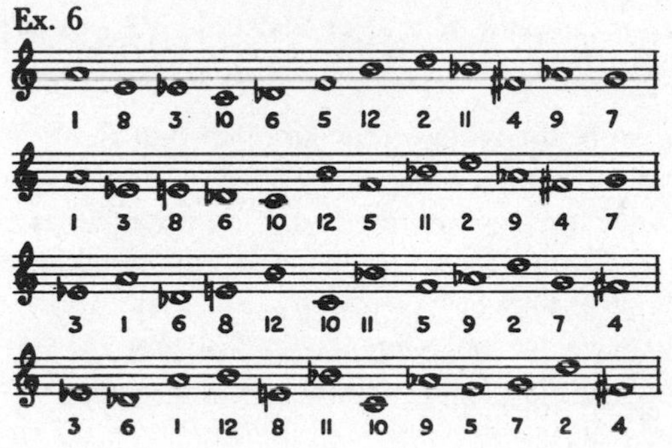

The term "mirror" finally refers to the fact that the musical configuration that opens the work and is expressed in terms of the row O1 returns in inverted form when the serial "conveyor belt" produces the form I 1, in retrograde inverted form when the row RI 1 appears (not shown in the above table), and at the very end of the work in terms of the form R 1. The remaining areas of the music are not any longer occupied by thematic statement, development, recapitulation, and the like. Whatever morphological kinship may be detected between adjacent sections is a result of similarities of intervallic shapes that may occur in neighboring forms of the tone-row, the vicinity of which, however, is a consequence of the premeditated serial arrangement outlined above and not dictated by requirements of a so-called musical nature.

In this composition no other parameter beside the succession of tones was serially ordered. In this respect it belongs to the province of "classical" twelve-tone music. It transcends that province in that it allows its structure to arise from the serial arrangement of the rotational derivatives of its tone-row.

The principle of rotation, which, as may be seen here, I discovered and utilized for reasons not relevant to the evolution of pan-parametrical organization, turned out to be of far-reaching significance when I became interested in that kind of organization. The point is that the notion of invariancy inherent by definition to the concept of the series, if applied to all parameters, leads to a uniformity of configurations that eliminates the last traces of unpredictability, or surprise. But unpredictability appears to be not only especially characteristic of so-called "atonal" music, but desirable, or necessary, in any work of art. That the composers who have made the most consistent attempts at "total determinacy" are aware of this need transpires from this utterance of Pierre Boulez: "L'inattendu, encore: il n'y a de création que dans l'imprévisible devenant nécessité."[5]

Combination of the various configurations that result from rotational procedure with constant (non-rotating) serial elements means that the principle of order that governs one set is applied to another, unrelated set (as if one, for instance, would order the numbers from 1 to 5 alphabetically: five four one three two). Since this is one of the definitions of randomness, we meet here for the first time the factor of chance, which has attained high significance in recent developments.

Rotation and Time

According to György Ligeti's analysis[6] of Pierre Boulez's *Structures* for two pianos,[7] the composer has interpreted the transpositions of his twelve-tone row to various pitch levels as a form of rotation and has transplanted the results to the parameter of time in order to obtain an analogous sequence of derivative forms of his time series.

[5] "The unexpected, again: there is no creation except in the unforseeable becoming necessary". (*Revue musicale,* April 1952, p. 119, as quoted in *Die Reihe,* No. 4, Vienna, 1958, p. 71). It is interesting that this statement almost *verbatim* sums up Carl Bricken's brilliant argument about "inevitability and the unexpected" in his analysis of Beethoven's Quartet Op. 18, No. 3 (*Some Analytical Approaches to Musical Criticism,* in *Proceedings of the Music Teachers National Association for 1936,* Oberlin, 1937, p. 262 ff.). In Bricken's discourse the "inevitable" is, of course, represented by those musical processes that appear to be most likely to occur within the framework of tonal harmony so that they constitute a predictable, "normal" set of events. The "unexpected," then, consists of the deviations from the norm introduced by the genius of the individual composer. In the case of serial music the inevitable is what serial premeditation ordains. The unexpected, however, is not a result of the composer's kicking against the self-imposed limitations, but of the built-in surprise mechanism, as we shall see later on. In my article *Is the Twelve-Tone Technique on the Decline?* (in *The Musical Quarterly,* Oct. 1953, p. 523 ff.) I indicated that Boulez in his Second Piano Sonata probably applied the principle of rotation.

[6] *Die Reihe,* No. 4, p. 38 ff.

[7] Universal Edition, Vienna.

The elements of the tone series are numbered from 1 to 12:

Ex. 7

1 2 3 4 5 6 7 8 9 10 11 12

To this a series of time values corresponds, expressed in terms of 𝅘𝅥𝅯𝅯 :

1 2 3 4 5 6 7 8 9 10 11 12

If we transpose the tone row, for instance, a major third higher, the original order of the tones is changed into:

Ex. 8

5 6 8 9 12 10 4 11 7 2 3 1

Correspondingly the time series would take on the shape:

5 6 8 9 12 10 4 11 7 2 3 1

In fact, the whole work consists of manifold combinations of the tone- and time-sets thus obtained.

Serialism in the Electronic Medium

Karlheinz Stockhausen's work described alternatingly as *Komposition 1953 No. 2* and *Elektronische Studie I*[8] is based on a six-tone series which according to the composer's own elaborate analysis[9] is an expression of this series of ratios of frequencies:

$$\frac{12}{5} \quad \frac{4}{5} \quad \frac{8}{5} \quad \frac{5}{12} \quad \frac{5}{4}$$

Expressed in vibration numbers, or cycles, per second, the first series reads:

1920	800	1000	625	1500	1200
12 :	5	8 :	5	5 :	4
	4 :	5	5 :	12	

In notes it reads approximately:

Ex. 9

Five more series are derived by making the consecutive tones of the first series points of departure for new series identically built (a procedure somewhat reminiscent of my *Lamentatio* rotation):

800	333	417	260	625	500
1000	417	521	325	781	625
625	260	325	203	488	390
1500	625	781	488	1170	937
1200	500	625	390	937	750

[8] Universal Edition, Vienna. Recorded by the Deutsche Grammophon Gesellschaft.

[9] *Technische Hausmitteilungen des Nordwestdeutschen Rundfunks,* Vol. VI, No. 1/2, Cologne, 1954, Item 10, p. 46 ff.

A second set of six series is obtained by making the second line of the first set the top line of the new set, then the third, and so on.

All parameters are serially ordered in terms of some variants of the numerical sequence 1 to 6. For instance, the combinations of the above frequencies follow from the series 4 5 3 6 2 1 in that the first tone-combination (*"Tongemisch"*) has four tones, the second five, and so on. There are four such *"Gemische"* in "sequence 1" (a "sequence" being a grouping of consecutive elements), and four "sequences" in the first "structure," which is the next higher compound, "horizontal" or "vertical." (It does not become quite clear on what grounds one or the other of these two dimensions was chosen.) There are six dynamic levels which are assigned to the various frequencies in proportion to their relative positions in the groups and columns of the entire system. The series that orders the succession of dynamic levels within this frame of reference is 3 4 2 1 6 5. Finally, the time factor is determined by relating the durations of the individual sounding elements to the pitch levels and degrees of loudness of those elements as ordered by the previous rules. The governing series in this parameter is 2 4 6 3 5 1.

The details of this organization are far more complex than what we are able to indicate here in an abridged sketch. Unfortunately the presentation by the author is not always felicitous, so that some of the intricacies of his work remain obscure. At any rate, the character of his reasoning seems to reveal a desire to derive the rules of serial organization from the nature of the chosen material and its intervallic texture. In this respect Stockhausen differs somewhat from Boulez, who has a rather mechanistic approach in assigning numerical values to the various magnitudes manipulated in his work. While this procedure of Boulez's has been criticized as "anorganic,"[10] it has nevertheless produced a fascinating piece of music. On the other hand, Stockhausen's *Studie,* although much shorter than the *Structures;* suffers from considerable monotony of harmonic flavor, which is due to the prevalence of augmented triads in the original series (see Ex. 9). The extraordinary subtleties of combinations of dynamic shadings, time values, echo effects, and the like cannot overcome this initial handicap.

The objection was raised that music here becomes the victim of an abstract numbers game which is contrary to the nature of music. While there undoubtedly is room for more than one definition of the nature of music, we did not extend our inquiry into this field. The numbers used

[10] Ligeti, *loc. cit.,* p. 41.

in the ordering of the parameters of serial music are almost always derived from proportions and measurements of the basic musical substance. Of course, these numbers detach themselves from the objects with which they were associated and take on a life of their own in the various operations performed. The results of these operations are, however, retranslated into musical terms and applied to the sounding material. In this relation of number and reality one may see a vague analogy to the connection of contemporary mathematics and physics.

Premeditated, but Unpredictable

In my oratorio for voices and electronic sounds, *Spiritus intelligentiae, sanctus,*[11] there is a section without voices (so to speak an "instrumental" interlude). The material of this section is a tempered scale of thirteen tones. From the continuum of this scale, groups of tones were selected to form alternatingly disjunct and conjunct heptachords of equal and symmetrical structure (see left side of Diagram 1). A seven-tone pattern (seven-tone row) meanders through this system of pitches constantly retaining its principle of progress: from any tone on which it starts it goes up to the third and fourth, then back to the second, up to the sixth, back to the fifth, and it stops on the seventh tone of the network of pitches. Since the pattern always progresses conjunctly (which means that the first tone of its next appearance is identical with the last of the preceding) while the pitch system is based on the alternation of conjunct and disjunct shapes, the internal intervallic configuration of the pattern is always different, although its general outline remains the same (see right side of Diagram 1). After thirteen appearances the pattern lands again on the tone from which it started, and the "rotation" has come to an end.

The interlude in question may technically be called a double canon. One of the two elements subject to imitation is a tone-line consisting of the chain of the thirteen possible variants of the seven-tone pattern just described, the other is an analogous line presenting the chain of the inverted forms of the pattern. The first tone-line is so designed that it begins on the central tone of the entire gamut (330 cycles), rises to its highest level (4754 c) in the first third of its length, returns to the center in the second third, and descends to the lowest level (26 c) in its last portion. The second line begins on the lowest point when the first reaches its apex, rises to cross the first line where it passes on its descent the central tone, goes up to its own high point which it reaches approximately when the first line ends, and returns to the center.

[11] Recorded by the Deutsche Grammophon Gesellschaft (LP 16134 Hi-Fi).

Diagram 1

Read from bottom up

Heavy lines indicate octaves

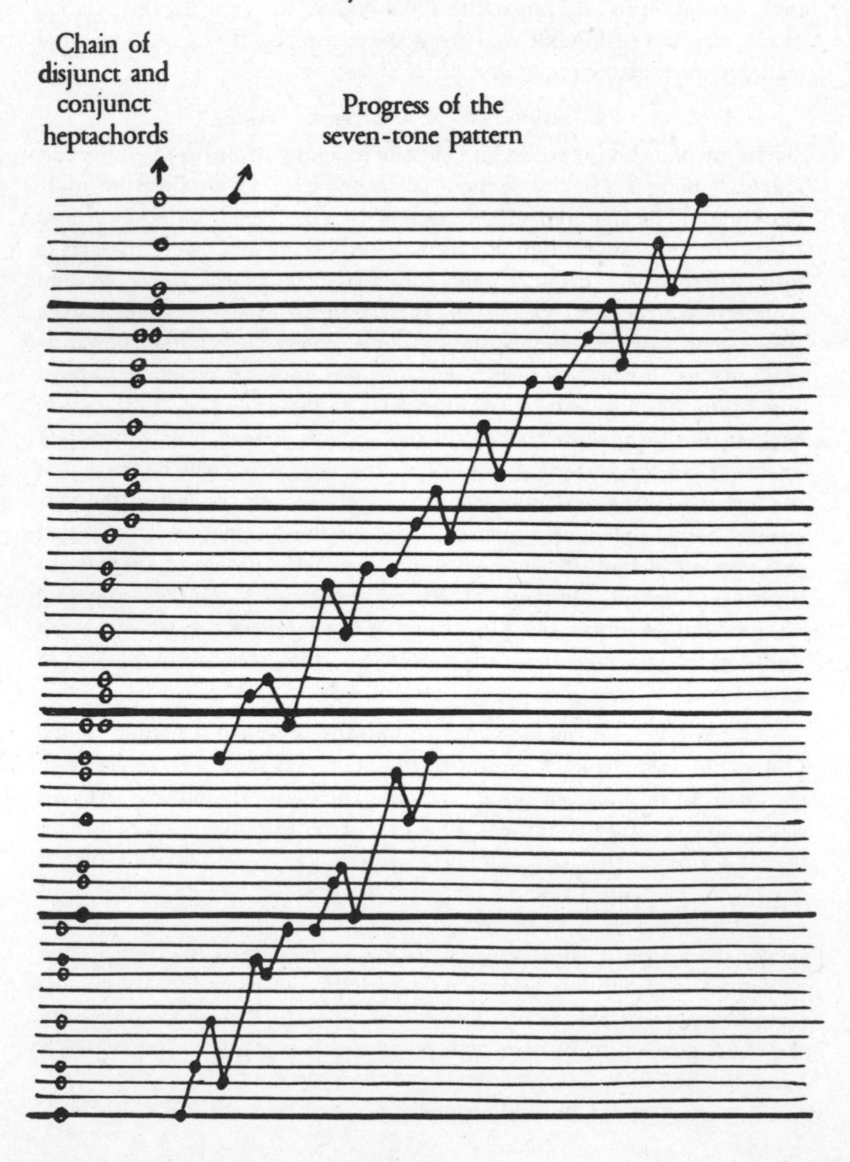

The canonic imitations were obtained by rerecording the original material at a higher and a lower speed, in which procedure the pitch level of the original tape was automatically raised or lowered in the same proportion. These imitations were so synchronized with the original lines that the slowed-down version of the ascending branch of the first tone-line would reach its highest point (proportionately lower than the summit of the original) when the original line had returned to the center. It was followed by the slowed-down imitation of the descending branch of the second line. The above-center arcs of both lines were imitated in accelerated versions reaching their (proportionately higher) apices shortly after or before those of the original lines. Finally, a very highly accelerated imitation of the below-center branches of both lines was inserted shortly before the end of the section.

To determine the time values of the single elements the whole expanse of the piece was viewed as one unit. Through measuring the linear distances of the important points of articulation — entrances of imitations, turning points and such — a series of eleven spans was established, a sort of macro-rhythm articulating the over-all structure. It was reduced in scale to a micro-rhythm in order to determine the durations of the individual tones in each tone-line. Since each line takes approximately three quarters of the entire length of the piece and each line contains ninety-one tones (seven times thirteen), the micro-rhythm of eleven values has to be repeated eight times, leaving three tones free at the end. This concept determined the ratio by which the macro-rhythm had to be reduced. Since the rhythmic series thus established has eleven terms whereas the tone-series has only seven tones, it follows that the last four terms of the first time series will apply to the first four tones of the second tone series, and so forth, so that here again mechanical repetition is avoided while uniformity in a higher sense is maintained. (See Diagram 2.)

It may be stated that whatever occurs in this piece at any given point is premeditated and therefore technically predictable. However, while the preparation and the layout of the material as well as the operations performed therein are the consequence of serial premeditation, the audible results of these procedures were not visualized as the purpose of the procedures. Seen from this angle, the results are incidental. They are also practically unpredictable because the simultaneous progress of highly complex rhythmic patterns at various relative speeds together with the corresponding transpositions of equally complex pitch patterns creates situations that defy precise visualization.

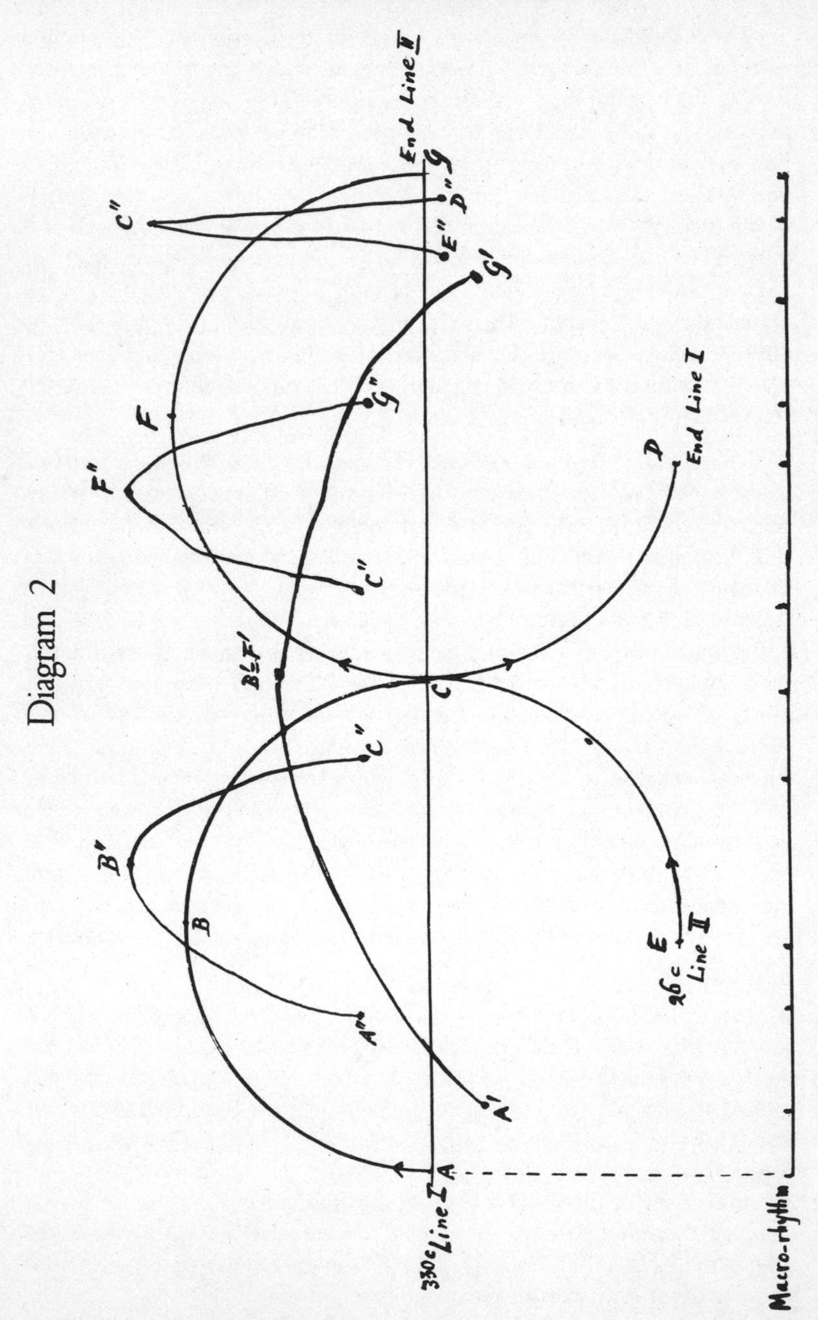
End Line III
End Line I
330c Line I
26c Line II
Macro-rhythm
A
A'
A"
B
B'
C
C"
D
D"
E
E"
F
F"
G
G'
G"
B♭=F'

Diagram 2

THE TIME MECHANISM OF MY "SESTINA"[12]

The *Sestina* is one of the poetic forms developed by the Provençal poets of the twelfth century, its original specimen being ascribed to Arnaut Daniel. It may well be called a serial form of poetry, and its essential formative principle is rotation.

The poem consists of six stanzas of six blank verses each. It hinges upon six keywords which appear at the endings of the individual lines. If in the first stanza the order of these words is 1 2 3 4 5 6, the words will appear in the second stanza in the order 6 1 5 2 4 3. The principle of rotation which is applied here consists in switching the position of every two keywords equidistant from the center of the series, proceeding from the end toward the middle. According to the same principle, the positions of the keywords in the subsequent stanzas are 3 6 4 1 2 5; 5 3 2 6 1 4; 4 5 1 3 6 2; 2 4 6 5 3 1. The process ends here, since the next rotation would produce the original series. The six stanzas are followed by a *Tornada* of three lines in which the keywords, one of each pair in the middle and the other at the end of the line, appear in the order 2 5, 4 3, 6 1.

The content of the *Sestina* which I wrote (in German) as text for the present composition is a contemplation of the implications of the idea governing the musical construction of the work.[13]

The first two stanzas may suffice to indicate the character and form of the poem:

1. Vergangen Klang und Klage, sanfter Strom.
   Die Schwingung der Sekunde wird zum Mass.
   Was in Geschichte lebt, war's nur ein Zufall?
   Verfall, Verhall, zerronnene Gestalt?
   Die Stunde zeitigt Wandel, wendet Zeit.
   Das Vorgeschrittne ordnet sich der Zahl.

2. In Schritten vorgeordnet durch die Zahl
   gestaltet sich Gedanke, doch zum Strom
   wird strenge Teilung, uhr-genaue Zeit.
   Ist es vermessen, solches Mass von Mass
   dem Leben aufzuzwingen, der Gestalt?
   Der Zwang zerrinnt, erzeugt den neuen Zufall.[14]

[12] Bärenreiter-Verlag, Kassel. Epic Records, LC 3509.

[13] Quoted from my notes on the jacket of the record cited in note 12.

[14] In a nearly literal translation which reproduces the positions of the key words:

> Bygone are sound and mourning, tender stream.
> Vibration of the second becomes the measure.
> What lives in history, was it only chance?
> Decline, fading sound, vanished shape?
> The hour causes change, turns the time.
> What looks ahead subordinates itself to number.

The music of my *Sestina* is based on a twelve-tone row divided into two groups of six tones each:

The figures indicate the size of the intervals measured in half-steps. These tone-rows are rotated according to the principle of the sestina so that the second A- and B-groups read:

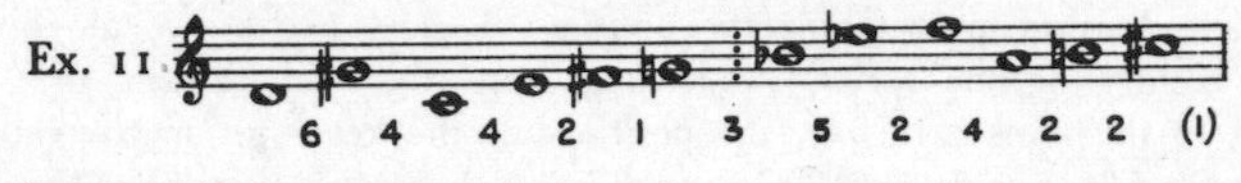

The third line is:

Ex. 12

5 4 2 4 4 1 3 1 4 6 4

and so forth. The tones are always placed so that they will not exceed the ambitus of the original row and the intervals (indicated by the numbers below the staff) are so measured up or down that their magnitudes will not exceed the figure 6. Obviously the sequence of these intervallic magnitudes constantly changes as a result of the rotation of the tones prescribed by the sestina pattern, but these changes are of a different order.

The durations of the tones of the whole composition are derived from these magnitudes in the following manner: each intervallic magnitude corresponds to a time segment which contains as many basic time units as the interval figure indicates. Consequently the first time segment has four units, the second three, etc. Each segment has as many tones as it has units (4, 3, etc.). The duration of the individual tones is determined by a subdivision based on the same serial sequence of magnitudes. If the first segment contains four units and four tones, its subdivision is based on the first four values of the original series: 4 3 1 6. The sum of these being 14, the subdivision unit within the first segment is 4/14. The durations of the individual tones within the first segment are determined by multiplying 4/14 consecutively by 4, 3, 1, and 6. The

In stages preordained by number
thought takes shape, but a stream
is (the result of) strict division, of clocklike, precise time.
Is it presuming to force such an extent of measure
on life, on shape?
Force vanishes, brings forth new chance.

durations, then, are 16/14, 12/14, and 24/14, or 8/7, 6/7, 2/7, and 12/7 of the basic value.

Actually the determination of the durations is due to much more complicated computation because it is influenced by serial organization of other parameters. In order to achieve higher rhythmic diversity, the concept of "internal speed" was introduced. It is derived from the assumption that in every group of six tones one to five tones might be sounded an octave higher so that the magnitude of the affected intervals would be augmented by twelve. The succession of "internal speeds" is derived from the position of the tones in group B (see Ex. 10). The lowest (A) is designated as 1, the highest (F) as 6. The initial row of internal speeds is therefore 5 1 4 3 6 2. The first segment, then, has the internal speed 5 so that 12 is added to five out of six subdivision numbers. Thus these numbers read 16 15 13 18 14 instead of 4 3 1 6 2. The following number — 1 — remains unaltered. The sum of the numbers attached to the first segment is therefore 62, instead of 14. Consequently the durations of the individual tones will be considerably shorter than if the "internal speed" were, for instance, 1 or 2.

To facilitate computations each basic unit is assumed to contain ten micro-units. We arrive at the subdivision of the first segment by dividing 40 (four times ten) by 62. The result is 0.645. This number is multiplied consecutively by 4, 3, 1, 6. The results are 2.58, 1.935, 0.645, 3.87. If the work had been realized by electronic means on tape, these values could be produced with utmost accuracy. Since it was conceived for conventional manners of rendition, the time values had to be adjusted as follows: 2.5, 2, 0.5, 4. If the smallest numerical unit is expressed by 𝅘𝅥𝅯 , the rhythmic shape of the first four tones is 𝅘𝅥𝅮‿𝅘𝅥𝅰 𝅘𝅥𝅯.‿♬ 𝅘𝅥𝅮.‿𝅘𝅥𝅯 = 9/16.

"Density" is the next parameter to be determined serially. There are six degrees of density whose succession is determined by the position of the pitches in group A (Ex. 10). Again the lowest (C) is called 1, the highest (G♯) 6. Consequently the initial series of densities is 6 3 5 4 1 2. In "density 1" the two tone-groups A and B run off simultaneously in a sort of two-part setting in which the duration of the individual tones is determined by the mechanism described above. In "density 2" the first and second time segments of group A run concurrently with the first segment of group B. In "density 3" two segments of each group are developed simultaneously, and so forth, until in "density 6" six segments of each group, i.e. twelve all together, run off at the same time.

Another parameter is the location of the tones within the gamut of six octaves designated as the ambitus of the work. The serial statement adopted for this area reads that the tones of each segment should run through as many octaves as there are tones. The direction of the motion is determined by the direction of the corresponding interval in the original series. Since many segments contain less than six tones, they cover less than six octaves and therefore could extend over various bands of the complete ambitus. This, too, is regulated by special serial statements. Needless to say that all these serial organisms are subject to rotation according to the sestina pattern, which is the supreme law governing every move of every variable within the whole composition.

The structural layout is designed to combine each "rotated" version of any six-tone group with every other. Thus the music of the first stanza is based on the first statement of the A-group, in each consecutive line of the poem combined with one of the forms of the B-group rotated from B 1 to B 6. The second stanza has A 2, combined again with all six B-groups, but now in a different sequence, according to the sestina pattern: B 6, B 1, B 5, B 2, B 4, B 3.

Paralleling the arrangement of the key words in the *tornada,* the tone series assigned to it reads 2 5 4 3 6 1. The music of the tornada consists of six sections, the first four and the last of which are given over to the instruments alone. While the tone row of the tornada undergoes the now familiar six sestina transformations, the density increases from 1 to 6 so that in the first section of the tornada only one each of the A- and B-rows are employed, while in the last section six of each, that is twelve, or all available forms are used simultaneously.

The parameter of "external speed" has six steps also, the lowest being M ♪ = 90, the highest ♪ = 180. The former is associated with the highest degree of density, the latter with the lowest.

Example 13 shows the first ten sixteenths (micro-units) which form the first basic time unit of the *Sestina.* On the left side one may see the distribution of the tones of the A- and B-groups over the twelve layers (density 6) of simultaneously progressing time segments, each tone entering at the point assigned to it by the time mechanism explained above. The tones occupy their places from top to bottom layer in their order of succession in the row. The "internal speed" for the A-layers (top six) is 5, for the B-layers (bottom six) 1 (no acceleration). Encircled numbers indicate the number of tones allotted to the particular segments. Arrows indicate the direction of the tone lines. The figures above the top staff give the durations of the first four tones in ♪, as computed on p. 225. The right side of the example shows how these tones are represented in the actual score, and a few connecting lines were drawn to demonstrate where some particular tones may be found.

Ex. 13

It is easy to see that the parameter of timbre lies beyond the limits of the present serial arrangement. If this parameter too were organized serially and this procedure would, for instance, require the first tone of the top layer (G♯) to be played by the trumpet, it would obviously be at variance with the octave register demanded by the serial regulation of spacing, since the trumpet cannot play the G♯ in question.

The Element of Chance

Other parameters may be affected in the same way. If the succession of tones is determined by serial regulation (as is the case in the classical twelve-tone technique) and, in addition to this, the timing of the entrance into the musical process of these tones is also predetermined by serial calculation (as, for example, in the case of the *Sestina*), it is no longer possible to decide freely (that is, by "inspiration") which tones should sound simultaneously at any given point. In other words, the so-called harmonic aspect of the piece will be entirely the result of operations performed on premises that have nothing to do with concepts of "harmony," be it on the assumption of tonality or atonality or anything else. Whatever happens at any given point is a product of the preconceived serial organization, but by the same token it is a chance occurrence because it is as such not anticipated by the mind that invented the mechanism and set it in motion.

Generally and traditionally "inspiration" is held in great respect as the most distinguished source of the creative process in art. It should be remembered that inspiration by definition is closely related to chance, for it is the very thing that cannot be controlled, manufactured, or premeditated in any way. It is what falls into the mind (according to the German term *Einfall*), unsolicited, unprepared, unrehearsed, coming from nowhere. This obviously answers the definition of chance as "the absence of any known reason why an event should turn out one way rather than another."[15] Actually the composer has come to distrust his inspiration because it is not really as innocent as it was supposed to be, but rather conditioned by a tremendous body of recollection, tradition, training, and experience. In order to avoid the dictations of such ghosts, he prefers to set up an impersonal mechanism which will furnish, according to premeditated patterns, unpredictable situations. Ligeti characterizes this state of affairs very well: "We stand in front of a row of slot machines ["*Automaten*"] and we can choose freely into which one we want to drop our coin, but at the same time we are forced to choose one of them. One constructs his own prison according to his wishes and is afterwards equally freely active within those walls — that is: not entirely free, but not totally constrained either. Thus automation does not function as the opposite of free decision: rather free selection and

[15] *The American College Dictionary,* New York and London, 1948, p. 200.

mechanization are united in the process of selecting the mechanism."[16] In other words, the creative act takes place in an area in which it has so far been entirely unsuspected, namely in setting up the serial statements (selecting the slot machines). What happens afterwards is predetermined by the selection of the mechanism, but not premeditated except as an unconscious result of the predetermined operations. The unexpected happens by necessity. The surprise is built in.

Layers and Densities

A later serial work of mine is a set of six piano pieces, called *Sechs Vermessene*. This German title is a play on words, since *vermessen* in German means "completely measured" as well as "presuming," a pun that cannot be reproduced in English. While the time mechanism is similar to that of the *Sestina,* the construction differs from it in that for the first three pieces a system of five layers is set up in which the first has "density 1" (i.e. one tone at a time), the next has two tones together, the third three, the fourth four, and the fifth six tones. The time measurements for the various layers are a result of summing up the interval magnitudes involved in the consecutive tone combinations. For example, the tone series of this composition being:

Ex. 14

the first combination of tones in "density 2" is:

Ex. 15

The numerical values derived from this progression are 3 (a minor third from G to B♭) and 1 (a half-step from E to F). Consequently the first time segment of the first layer has three units, the first of the second has four (3 + 1). As the density of the layers increases, the number of simultaneously sounding intervals and thus the numerical values of their sums become higher. Therefore the time segments become longer, which means that the chords, or tone-clusters, with increasing thickness are spaced farther apart, while the single tones of the first layer follow each other more rapidly. Computations of this kind form the basis of the whole composition.

As explained before, phenomena in the parameter of harmony must be accepted as results of the operations in the sectors of pitch succession and time. In the fourth of the piano pieces an attempt was made to

[16] *Loc. cit.*, p. 38 (translated from the German by this writer).

begin with a selection of sound elements. From the tone row we developed twelve sets of four elements each (consisting of one, or of two, three, or four tones played simultaneously) plus two six-tone chords. These fifty elements were numbered from 1 to 50 and their succession was determined by progressing along this series by the distances indicated in the numerical values of the intervals of the basic row:

series of elements:	1	2	3	4.	5	6	7	8	9	10	11	12	13	14	15	...
intervals of the tone row:	3			2		5					4					...
selected elements:	1			4		6					11				15	...

In the fifth piece the five degrees of thicknesses (see above) are distributed over five layers which progress at various speeds so that the time measurements of the slowest layer are reduced to 1/2 in the second, to 1/3 in the third, to 1/4 in the fourth, and to 1/6 in the fastest layer.

Progressively Varying Series

In the field of serial music one may observe a tendency towards using series of magnitudes that progressively vary according to some serial ordering of their own. The speed levels of the *Sestina* are an example. Another time series of this nature was established for the voice line of this work. It is based on the succession of 1 2 3 5 7 and 10 ♪ for the accented syllables. The opening succession is 2 3 10 5 7 1 and the following forms are obtained through the sestina rotation. Since each line of the poem has only five accented syllables, interesting situations of overlaps occur.

It may be seen that the series here applied is a modification of the so-called Fibonacci series in which each term is equal to the sum of the two preceding terms: 1 2 3 5 8 13 21 34 55 etc.[17] Luigi Nono has used the first six terms of this series as factors with which he multiplies the basic time values of his *Il Canto sospeso* in order to obtain the actual durations of the individual tones.[18] I have used the terms of the Fibonacci series from 2 to 21 to determine the speed zones in a recent orchestral composition entitled *Quaestio temporis* (*A Question of Time*). This work is based on a twelve-tone row that contains all eleven intervals in this order (measured in half-steps):

3 8 5 10 11 6 1 2 7 4 9

The entire expanse of the composition is thought of as consisting of 66

[17] Cf. Matila Ghyka, *The Geometry of Art and Life*, New York, 1946, p. 13 f.

[18] Cf. Karlheinz Stockhausen's analysis of the work in *Darmstädter Beiträge zur neuen Musik*, Mainz, 1958, p. 70.

time units (the sum of the above figures), which form eleven sections of varying lengths according to the magnitudes of the basic series. To these sections six different speeds are assigned:

M ♩ = 20, 30, 50, 80, 130, and 210

The Concept of Density Generalized

It appears that density is a function of speed and thickness of texture. If the latter may be called the vertical component of density because it depends on how many layers are in operation at the same time, speed is the horizontal component of density since the tones follow each other more closely the faster the tempo of the music is. If both parameters approach maximum values, a degree of saturation is reached at which accurate computations of time points and durations become irrelevant. When in the final section of *Quaestio* twelve layers (maximum vertical density) progress at a speed of ♩ = 210 per minute, the tones come so close together that nearly every sixteenth is sounded, frequently by several tones simultaneously. The velocity of the music causes 14 𝅘𝅥𝅯 to run off per second. At this rate even the succession of pitches is not any longer of great significance. It seems sufficient to determine by experiment within a limited area the average number of time units needed for running through the twelve-tone series. The results of this statistical examination are then used in order to fill this area of highest density with actual musical sounds.

What Does Serial Music "Mean," if Anything?

One of the parameters that obviously cannot be controlled by premeditation when those so far discussed are subjected to serial ordering is the expressive, or communicative, aspect of music. If a serial composer were concerned with this problem, he would have to set up a series of "moods," or "ideas," or something of this sort, to begin with, and then let the other parameters fall in line. It so happens that serial composers are not thinking in such terms.

In a more pessimistic attitude than he now seems to entertain, the German composer and philosopher, T. W. Adorno, has criticized the recent developments of serial music[19] because in these the (according to him) deep-rooted and essential analogy and affinity of music and speech is abandoned. While it may be true that music from the time of plainchant has been oriented towards speech-like articulation, diction, and over-all structure, and while especially the exploits of Expressionism and

[19] *Das Altern der neuen Musik,* in *Der Monat,* May 1955.

atonality point to a very close association with the free articulation of prose, we have to face the fact that under the influence of the constructive rigor that was the very consequence of Expressionistic roaming serial music has turned away from its rhetorical past. Since whatever music seems to communicate is not so much the supposed content of the audible matter as it is the product of the listener's reaction touched off by his auditory experience, there is no reason to assume that the nature of serial music excludes the possibility of interpreting it as a medium of some sort of communication. The interest it may evoke is similar to that elicited by the process of life, to which serial music is related in the paradox of the chaotic appearance of totally and systematically traceable causality. It may mean as much or as little as life itself.

BARTOK'S "SERIAL" COMPOSITION

By ALLEN FORTE

IN 1928, when Schoenberg's serial concept was beginning to exhibit the rapidity and diversity of development now regarded as characteristic, Bartók devoted the third movement of his Fourth String Quartet to the extended and elaborate expression of a relational system that closely resembles a serial schema. It must be added immediately that although this composition is clearly exploratory it is not imitative either of Schoenberg or of his students; rather, the system upon which it is based arises as a logical consequence of tonal materials unique to the Fourth Quartet. Necessary further qualification of the term "serial" may be deduced from the analysis given below.

Because of Bartók's reluctance to discuss details of compositional technique, we are left in doubt as to the precise extent of his knowledge of serial procedures.[1] But whatever this might have been, the third movement of the Fourth Quartet stands as an extraordinary demonstration of his ability to employ diverse and seemingly contradictory procedures without sacrificing either the integrity or the unique characteristics of his music. In addition, the work testifies to Bartók's compositional prowess, for it offers cogent solutions to certain harmonic problems of non-triadic music, solutions matched only later by avowedly twelve-tone composers.

The iterative, symmetrical nature of the Fourth Quartet as a whole is not reflected lucidly by the surface of the third movement. However, careful listening reveals that beyond its highly improvisational exterior

[1] With reference to the Fourth Quartet and other works, Halsey Stevens writes of "certain characteristics presumably conditioned by Bartók's acquaintance with the music of Schoenberg and Stravinsky" (*The Life and Music of Béla Bartók,* New York, 1953, p. 205).

lies a system of relations that integrates every detail. A representation of this system is provided by Ex. 1.[2]

The pair of notes that spans the interval of a major second (hereafter referred to as the whole-tone dyad, or simply dyad) is primal to the system. The fundamental principle by which the system is generated from the dyad is complementation: the combining of symmetrically related structural elements, both with and without overlapping, to form a higher unity. Thus the dyad gives rise to a trichord, a group of three contiguous notes spanning a major third (e.g., element *w* in sub-system I of Ex. 1), and the trichord, in turn, generates a threefold system of hexachords, hexachords of three distinct yet interrelated species: sub-system I contains the two whole-tone hexachords, *wx* and *yz,* which constitute the axis of the entire system; sub-system II contains six "diatonic" hexachords constructed in ascending pitch-order from each note of *wx,* while sub-system III contains six diatonic hexachords similarly constructed from *yz.* Whereas no special device seems required to show the complementary relation between the two whole-tone hexachords of sub-system I (with respect to the total ordering of twelve pitch-classes), beams are used in sub-systems II and III to identify complementary hexachords of the diatonic species.

It is evident that the whole-tone axis (I) includes all the trichords that compose the diatonic hexachords of sub-systems II and III. The

[2] Ex. 1 stresses the iterative rather than the symmetrical characteristic of the system in order to show more directly the constituent hexachordal species explained below.

axial nature of the whole-tone hexachords is confirmed when by combining *w* and *y* or *x* and *z* we obtain the third species of hexachord, the chromatic hexachord. From the complementary relation between *wx* and *yz* it follows that *wy* complements *xz*.

The compositional potential of the system is indicated by the fact that a given trichord can combine with any of five discrete trichords to form a diatonic, whole-tone, or chromatic hexachord. By this means ordered expansion through the entire system is feasible. However, analysis demonstrates that Bartók imposed a specific limitation upon expansion by assigning a regulatory function to the trichord C-D-E, the element that represents the tonality of the entire Fourth Quartet. Therefore, although the composition is based upon a schema that has the properties of a twelve-tone system,[3] its development is determined not by those properties but by a non-serial element, the tonality-representing trichord C-D-E. The following analytic account of the movement amplifies this thesis with the aid of a synopsis of hexachordal combination and progression over the entire span of the movement:

Ex. 2

In order to represent the main harmonic succession as concisely as possible the synopsis (Ex. 2) provides only the boundary notes of trichords and hexachords and shows only those melodic elements that influence the over-all progression. The latter as well as certain secondary harmonic elements are represented by black noteheads.

The movement is divided into three large sections, designated by double bars in Ex. 2. Formal divisions both of long and short duration

[3] Bartók's system has quite special properties indeed: its hexachordal species represent three of the six possible "all-combinatorial" hexachords described by Milton Babbitt in *Some Aspects of Twelve-Tone Composition*, in *The Score*, XII (1955), 53-62.

coincide with changes of hexachordal combination, i.e., progression. These are clearly marked by changes of register, dynamics, and tempo, as well as by idiomatic string effects. The first 46 measures of the movement consist of an accompanied solo melody. In the remaining 25 measures two instruments are melodic while the other two provide accompaniment. During the early stages of the analysis it was assumed that the accompanying parts carried the more stable elements, the hexachordal or harmonic progression over the longer span, whereas the melody, in addition to identifying the hexachordal combination of the accompaniment, expressed more diversified relations. For this reason it seemed advantageous to divide the analytic account into two parts, the first dealing with the over-all harmonic progression, the second with the melody.

In the first section, mm. 1-40, the controlling element, the C trichord, is located within the C hexachord,[4] which is unfolded in "retrograde"[5] motion in the lower register after the manner of a *cantus firmus*. The temporal position of the C trichord within this *cantus firmus* affords it maximal control while allowing it the possibility of maximal association with other trichords by virtue of complementarity. Thus at the very outset the unfolding F trichord of the *cantus firmus* combines with the A trichord to form a whole-tone pentachord (*yz*). (The one note, E♭, that would complete the hexachord *yz* is omitted, for reasons that will be elaborated below.) Similarly, the C trichord of the *cantus firmus* combines with the E trichord to form a second whole-tone pentachord (*wx*), omitting B♭. Although the *cantus firmus* is to be regarded as generative, in the way just described, the E hexachord, comprising E and A trichords, assumes temporal priority over it and is stated in retrograde form at the beginning of the movement. In accord with the principle of complementation this hexachord seeks to incorporate the B♭ hexachord to form the highest unity: the ordering of the total chromatic, i.e., a twelve-tone set. It now becomes evident that complementation is the basis of progression from section to section and of hexachordal combination within each section. Consequently, the redirection or restriction of a potentially complementary progression or combination is

[4] For the sake of convenience a trichord or hexachord will be designated throughout by its lowest note, and "hexachord" refers to the diatonic species unless otherwise indicated.

[5] The structure of all three species of hexachord is such that only two of the customary operations obtain; therefore in this, to an even greater extent than in other instances, the designation of prime, retrograde, etc. is somewhat arbitrary. Because of the way in which the hexachordal schema is represented by Ex. 1 it seems preferable to designate the ascending form of the diatonic hexachord as prime.

an event of singular importance, one that must be specially indicated in the analytic synopsis (Ex. 2). Thus the E♭ trichord at m. 35 is enclosed in parentheses to show that although it occurs it is not defined in terms of the B♭ hexachord. (In this instance the melodic detail that effects redefinition of the E♭ trichord is not shown.) In amplification — and as further demonstration of the fundamental role of the trichord — we note that whereas trichordal complementation is consistently effected, hexachordal complementation is not, with the single exception of an instance involving whole-tone hexachords within a section controlled by diatonic hexachords (mm. 60-61, described below). The consistent preparation of complementary relationships, followed by their negation or redirection, suggests that Bartók regarded complementation as equivalent to closure of the system, and that he wished to avoid closure in order to permit the C trichord to remain unequivocally the fundamental element.

From this it follows that complementation is carefully controlled at every level of detail and over every temporal span. Thus, in the first section trichords are stated in such a way as to insure optimal clarity of relatedness. For example, the statement of the B♭ trichord at m. 22 coincides with the closure of the F trichord of the *cantus firmus,* making evident the "diatonically" complementary relation between them. Had the B♭ trichord appeared earlier it would have been understood only in its chromatically complementary relation to the A trichord or in its whole-tone relation to the E trichord. Moreover, since at this juncture the B♭ trichord relates directly to the E, A, and F trichords (complementing them to form whole-tone, chromatic, and diatonic hexachords, respectively), it serves as a precise measurement of expansion from the beginning of the movement.

As a further means of assuring coherent progression, the integrity of the *cantus firmus*'s trichords is carefully preserved. This is apparent from the outset, for after the *cantus firmus* moves to G (m. 13), B and only B is omitted from the melody during approximately five measures since it would tend to identify G of the *cantus* with the G trichord, B and G being the definitive terms thereof, and thus conflict with the essential placement of G within the F trichord which controls the harmonic succession over the longer span.

A relation of shorter span, but one that further integrates the work around the C trichord, is expressed at m. 32 by the B trichord. This element, in addition to complementing the C trichord chromatically, connotes the F trichord via the axial whole-tone hexachord *yz* and thus doubly supports the continuity of the *cantus firmus.*

Above D and C of the *cantus firmus* (mm. 33 and 34) appear elements that denote the E and B♭ hexachords. Since these hexachords also appeared above the F trichord (mm. 1-31), their restatement here above the C trichord serves as an additional unifying factor. Of greater importance to the over-all succession is the fact that in both instances the B♭ trichord does not incorporate the E♭ trichord to form a diatonic hexachord, although in both instances complementation is prepared. The more significant of these is the second (mm. 34-40). Before amplifying this we remark that the E♭ trichord has a decisive function in the first section and indeed throughout since it completes the B♭ hexachord, which, in turn, complements the E hexachord generated by the *cantus firmus,* thus effecting a definitive closure with respect to the total chromatic. Analysis reveals the means by which the complementary progression prepared during mm. 34-40 is redirected at m. 41 so as simultaneously to avoid closure and to afford further extension through the hexachordal system.

At m. 35 the first violin states and repeats the dyad E♭-F in the upper register. At m. 40 the structural demand for G as final term of the trichord E♭-F-G is intensified, analogically, by a redistribution of the accompanying instruments which permits F♯ to be introduced in the accompaniment: this note completes the dyad E-F♯, which has the same location in the E trichord of the accompaniment as does the E♭-F dyad in the E♭ trichord implied by the melody. However, at m. 41, which is set off both from preceding and following sections by the instruction *tranquillo,* the E♭-F dyad is defined in terms of the D♭ hexachord. For the benefit of those who may still doubt that the composing-out of the unique schema represented by Ex. 1 required an act of cognition on the part of the composer, we point out that the D♭ hexachord is the one hexachord in the system that shares the E♭-F dyad and only that dyad with the B♭ hexachord.

Additional refinements become evident with study. For example, the notes of the dyad E♭-F are stated at m. 35 in ascending pitch-order; at m. 38 this order is reversed, cueing the redefinition of the dyad at

m. 41 in terms of the F-E♭-D♭ trichord (D♭ hexachord) as explained above. The initial motif at m. 42, E♭-D♭, further confirms the significance of this permutation.

With the shift to the D♭ hexachord at m. 41 the composition extends for the first time to sub-system III, the hexachords of which contain no discrete trichords (with respect to sub-system II) and which accordingly have greater possibilities for progression and combination than those of sub-system II, which are controlled by the C trichord. However, a specific limitation is placed upon these possibilities when the D♭ hexachord is combined with the D hexachord of sub-system II, as shown in Ex. 2 (m. 41), for the two hexachords share one and only one note, G♭, and consequently exclude one note, C. In consideration of the principle of complementation this suggests progression to the C and G♭ hexachords — and thus a return to sub-system II — a progression that subsequently is effected with the assistance of melodic elements to be explained below

To continue the survey of hexachordal progression and combination over the total span of the movement, we observe that complementation of the C and G♭ hexachords (mm. 47-51) does not occur definitively, for although the F trichord is present, it is stated in conjunction with B; as a result it registers as an element of the whole-tone hexachord *yz* formed by cross-related trichords from each diatonic hexachord.

The hexachordal combination at m. 52 (E and F hexachords) is analogous to that at m. 41 (D♭ and D hexachords). However, the progression from this to the following section (m. 55) is not analogous, since this would have resulted in a combination of the less "stable" hexachords (E♭ and A) from sub-system III, thus transcending the limitation placed upon the system by the fundamental C trichord. Accordingly, the short section that extends from m. 52 to m. 54 marks the limit of expansion. This is made perfectly clear when at m. 55 there begins a second unfolding of the *cantus firmus,* this time within a matrix that is at once more condensed and more elaborate than that of its formal counterpart, mm. 1-34. Even the *cantus firmus* is stated more intricately, in a melody carried by the 'cello. A regularity of metrical accent distinguishes the *cantus firmus* from other melodic elements in the passage: the first two dyads of the simultaneously unfolding trichords, A-E and G-D, begin on downbeats, while the closure of the trichord begins with F on the third beat of the measure, in accord with the definitional function assigned to that metrical position throughout the movement.

In this penultimate section all motion continues to be regulated by the C trichord. Thus, in mm. 55-60 the chromatically related C and B hexachords are expressed within a carefully-wrought imitative pattern above the *cantus firmus*. An even more complex formation begins at m. 60, where the *cantus firmus* is interrupted by a direct linear statement of the whole-tone hexachord *yz*. The counterpoint of this passage will be explained below.

To summarize, complementation is the basis of trichordal and hexachordal combination within each section and of progression from section to section. As we have seen, operation of this principle is regulated by a single trichord, with the result that progression over the longer span is limited primarily to the hexachords of sub-system II. However, additional resources of the system are exploited at the level of melodic detail, where a high degree of elaboration and integration is obtained. An account of this follows.

Just as a melodic element in a triadic composition derives its meaning from the triad, so does a melodic element in the present work derive its meaning from the trichord and from the higher unities the trichord generates. But because of the system's iterative nature the meaning of a particular melodic element is potentially multiple. The structure of the trichord and hexachord therefore is reflected in the various degrees of specificity with which an interval denotes a higher unity. Examples 4-16 catalogue and illustrate these denotations, beginning with those of the minor second and proceeding to the tritone. Even a relatively complete account of the melodic detail would far exceed the limits of the present article; therefore each interval-denotation is illustrated by only a single instance in the composition. At this juncture it must be remarked that melodic embellishments in the sense of non-structural elements do not occur. Each note has a structural task which can be described with precision in relation to the hexachordal schema.

Because of its axial position within the diatonic hexachord the minor second denotes diatonically complementary trichords.

The minor second may also designate a chromatic hexachord (Ex. 4b). Accordingly, the initial motif, the dyad D♯-D in m. 6:

denotes both the B♭ hexachord, which complements the E hexachord already stated, and the chromatic hexachord on B (*wy*), which contains the fundamental C trichord. Thus, with a single two-note motif the melody reveals the relational system and indicates the direction that expansion will take in the total movement. This dual meaning is confirmed when, in m. 7, C is stated, for it is the one note required to complete the chromatic hexachord *wy* (the remaining notes already being present in the accompaniment). Therefore, in sum, the two initial measures of melody shown in Ex. 5 present in descending pitch-order (repeated notes excluded) the three notes required to define the chromatic hexachord *wy:* D♯, D, and C.

It now becomes clear that the trichords of the E hexachord are presented non-contiguously in mm. 4-5 (upper staff in Ex. 5) in order that the interval of a minor third formed between them may provide a chromatic matrix for the motif D♯-D. At least two additional reasons for this "inversion" suggest themselves: 1) A, the lowest note of the upper trichord, is to serve as point of departure for the descending *cantus firmus* and therefore the entire upper trichord is placed below the lower trichord; 2) the separation of the trichords emphasizes their function as essential unities from which all expansion stems.

The major second has two possible meanings: lower or upper dyad of a trichord. In connection with Ex. 3 we considered an instance of the structural use of this ambivalence in order to redirect diatonic hexachordal progression. An example of the major second within a whole-tone hexachord is provided by the melody of the section that begins at m. 22. There, with the closure of the upper trichord of the *cantus firmus,* melodic expansion is expressed in terms of the hexachord *yz,* which contains the F trichord just completed in the lower register (cf. m. 60). Thus the melody features the following succession of dyads: A-B, C♯-D♯, and F-G. It also includes three notes from the complementary hexachord *wx:* F♯, D, and B♭. These symmetrically related (equidistant) notes serve as references to the B♭ and E trichords carried by the accompaniment.

Within the diatonic hexachord the minor third obviously does not occur between contiguous notes. However, between non-contiguous notes it occurs three times and accordingly designates one of three hexachords:

Ex. 6

At m. 41 is a significant instance of the third possibility. There the shift to the D♭ hexachord is denoted only by the minor third D♭-B♭ (Ex. 3). Subsequently the D♭ hexachord receives confirmation when more of its elements are included both in melody and accompaniment.

Since the chromatic hexachord contains three non-contiguous minor thirds, a given minor third can denote any of three different (but overlapping) chromatic hexachords:

Ex. 7

Clearly the minor third—or any other melodic interval—can occur in a situation where it is not determinant, where its denotative function is subordinate to that of other intervals. The brackets in Ex. 8 (m. 49) mark two such cases:

Ex. 8

Ex. 9 verticalizes the notes shown in Ex. 8 in order to demonstrate their symmetrical arrangement[6] around C.

Ex. 9

Further clarification is provided by Ex. 10:

Ex. 10

which shows the underlying trichordal structure of the figure and demonstrates that the bracketed skips in Ex. 8 come about as an incidental result of the whole-tone dyads. Observe, moreover, that Bartók has notated the skips as augmented seconds, not as minor thirds.

The major third denotes a trichord. From the fact that melodic occurrences of this interval are negligible we can conclude that the composer deliberately restricted its use to the harmonic dimension,

[6] Cf. George Perle, *Symmetrical Formations in the String Quartets of Béla Bartók*, in *The Music Review*, XVI (1955), 300-12.

thereby obtaining a measure of control over hexachordal progression and combination which, in view of the associative property of the trichord in this work, would have been difficult to match had the melodic major third been used more frequently.

The perfect fourth occupies three different positions in the diatonic hexachord and bounds the chromatic hexachord. Correspondingly it denotes one of four hexachords:

Ex. 11

At m. 63, terminal point of the *cantus firmus*:

the fourth B♭-E♭ above the final C denotes simultaneously the G♭ hexachord, which complements the hexachord of the *cantus,* and the B♭ hexachord, the upper trichord of which has a pivotal role in the subsequent and final section.

Of the three species only the whole-tone hexachord contains the tritone:

Ex. 13

In the case of the other two species the tritone occurs between complementary hexachords and thus denotes the total chromatic:

Ex. 14

The location of the same tritone in the corresponding structural position with respect to both these species indicates the interchangeability of complementary pairs of diatonic with complementary pairs of chromatic hexachords under certain conditions. This relationship appears to be exploited to a certain extent in the vertical distribution of the accompaniment.

The following example (m. 43) illustrates the influence that the harmonic combination can exert even upon the tritone:

Taken alone, the F♭-B♭ tritone connotes the whole-tone hexachord *wx*. However, with reference to the D and D♭ hexachords, the harmonic combination of this section, it specifies the cross-related G♭ and D trichords, stressing the fulcral position of G♭ (the only note common to both hexachords) within the pentachord formed by those trichords. Further, the dyadic relation between F♭ and G♭ suggests an analogous relation between B♭ and C. This analogy is made clear by the parallel accentual-grouping of the melody, here set off against the strong metrical accents of the accompaniment:

Ex. 16 

Since C is excluded by the harmonic combination, the dyad B♭-C is not realized within this section. However, with the progression to the G♭-C hexachord combination at m. 47, C, which is to be the primal melodic note of that section, is stated precisely in that rhythmic position relative to B♭ which is shown in Ex. 16. We can generalize from this instance to state that accentual grouping of the melody in the entire movement is designed to register interval relations that identify the particular harmonic combination and prepare for progression.

To generalize, then, regarding the melodic aspect of the work, it has been demonstrated that trichordal and hexachordal segments express relations between the larger harmonic units operative within a section, relations that are ordered with respect to the hexachordal system as a whole and serve to define harmonic combinations and prepare progression. A final instance of this, perhaps the most extraordinary of all, is provided by the closing section, mm. 64-71, where the meaning of the B♭ trichord, stated melodically by the first violin, seems to be equivocal. However, an inventory of the whole-tone dyads featured by the 'cello melody—which appears to draw every possible implication from the B♭ trichord of the first violin—reveals that only one note is omitted, E♭. Thus, of the five possible trichords with which the B♭ trichord could be associated only one is not made explicit, the E♭ trichord, for combined with the B♭ trichord this would form a complete B♭ hexachord and thus close the system by effecting complementation of the E hexachord. The final melodic note of the movement, D, therefore is to be understood in terms of the whole-tone hexachord *wx*, a relationship made unequivocal by the final note of the accompaniment with which it sounds, G♯. More specifically, D and G♯ serve as final reference to the fundamental C trichord, which is contained within the hexachord *wx*. The selection of these particular notes to represent the whole-tone hexachord is explained by the fact that they served as points of departure for the accompaniment and melody, respectively, of the entire movement. Further, if we assume that the hexachord *wx* comprises the C and F♯ trichords as discrete components—which is reasonable in view of the primal function of the C trichord—and if we observe the analogous axial positions that D and G♯ occupy in those trichords, it becomes evident that these notes represent a summation of the relational system and of the principle of complementation by which the system was developed compositionally.

In addition to the trichordal and hexachordal segments, the melody carries some relatively complete statements of diatonic hexachords. In every case these express ordered relations between the total movement and the main harmonies of the particular section. Perhaps the most intricate illustration of this is provided by mm. 60-63, where the first violin and 'cello move in stretto, incorporating relatively complete statements of the A, C♯, F♯, and G hexachords. Since trichordal associations are maximal here, the hexachordal figures split into their component trichords, group around the whole-tone axis—directly unfolded in the inner parts—, and derive their structural meaning from it. The whole-tone hexachord, however, is exclusively a local event; in the context of the entire section (mm. 55-63) it serves to expand the unfolding *cantus firmus* as described above in connection with Ex. 2. Moreover, this whole-tone hexachord (*yz*) does not contain the C trichord, and therefore does not anticipate the termination of the *cantus firmus,* but, rather, prolongs it under conditions perfectly in accord with the symmetrical system of hexachords regulated by the *cantus firmus*.

The density of this penultimate passage stands in marked contrast to others in the movement, while the plasticity of the trichord which is evident there and which clearly makes of it the developmental apex, brings us to a final realization of the structural necessity for the limitations imposed upon detail—in the form of melodic permutations, ellipses, and accentual groupings, all of which represents Bartók's virtuosity in composition. But beyond this, the refined techniques demonstrated by every measure of the work testify to his musical versatility and perspicacity, attributes all the more remarkable in view of his uncompromising individuality. In the final analysis it is these intangibles that guarantee his position among the titans of modern music.

TWELVE-TONE INVARIANTS AS COMPOSITIONAL DETERMINANTS

By MILTON BABBITT

AT the present moment, when many of the jagged edges of abruption have been smoothed by time and practice, there are those who — presumably in the spirit of mediation and moderation — would minimize, not so much Schoenberg's achievement as a composer, as the degree to which the twelve-tone system is genuinely "revolutionary" in its nature and implications, the degree to which it imposes new demands of perception and conception upon the composer and listener, and — therefore — the degree to which it admits of further and extensive exploration and discovery.

Such an attitude does a disservice not only to Schoenberg, but to the cause of understanding, particularly since it so often involves the invocation of the alleged historical-analogical origins of the operations of the system, along with conjectures as to Schoenberg's mode of and motivation for arriving at the system. However intriguing such conjectures may be, they are as irrelevant as they are futile; however pedagogically convenient and intuitively suggestive a quasi-genetic approach may be, eventually it succeeds only in obscuring both the character of the system and the profound differences between the twelve-tone system and those musical systems in which the "historical forerunners" of the twelve-tone operations appear. The crucial point here is that these "forerunners" are not independent and fundamental structural determinants, but means of immediate procedure, neither necessarily present nor, if present, of more than local significance and influence.

Therefore it is appropriate to precede even so informal a discussion as the one to follow with the reminder that the twelve-tone system, like any formal system whose abstract model is satisfactorily formulable, can be characterized completely by stating its elements, the stipulated relation or relations among these elements, and the defined operations upon the so-related elements. Such a characterization, though explicitly presented in verbal form at the earliest stage of the twelve-tone development, is likewise easily and explicitly inferable as the maximum procedural intersection among the "classical" twelve-tone works of Schoenberg, Webern, and Berg.

If the elements of the twelve-tone pitch system are, indeed, "traditional" ones, both insofar as they are pitch classes with class membership defined by octave equivalence, and as there are twelve such pitch classes —corresponding to the chromatically equal-tempered quantization of the frequency continuum—even here essential deviations must be noted. In the twelve-tone system there is a one-to-one correlation between pitch notation and presented pitch, as opposed to the many-to-one correlation of triadic-tonal music; there can be no such distinctions as those between explicit and functional "dissonance," or between enharmonically identical "consonance" and "dissonance." The independent assumption of octave equivalence has been a frequent point of attack upon the system, particularly by those who assert that the corresponding assumption in the tonal system serves to define classes of equivalent function; it need be answered only that, similarly, this assumption in the twelve-tone system serves to define classes of equivalent order position.

It is in the definition of relations among the elements that the system diverges significantly from systems of the past, for relations are defined entirely by the imposition of a total linear ordering upon the pitch classes, thus defining a twelve-tone "set" (designated: S). The ordering employed, in any given work, is inferable from—at most—all of the compositional presentations of the set (and its transformations), and not necessarily from any one compositional presentation. By introducing this principle as the basis of relationship, Schoenberg not only effected a fusion of the general systematic constraint with the contextually defined property—for, although the principle of formation is defined for all sets, the specific pitch class relations defined by a set are uniquely associated with it and its transformations — but established the means of a permutational musical system, as opposed to the combinational systems of the past. Given a collection of available elements, the choice of a sub-collection of these as a referential norm provides a norm that is distinguishable by content alone; such a system, and the traditional tonal system is such, is therefore combinational. But if the referential norm is the totality of elements, there is but one such norm in terms of content, and deviations from this norm cannot exist within the system. But if an ordering is imposed upon this totality, and taken as a norm, this norm is so distinguished, in the case of twelve pitch class elements, from the 12![1] — 1 other possible orderings, that is, other possible permutations.

Any consideration of the operations of the system must proceed from an awareness of their permutational nature. As a simple example: transposition, excepting the identity transposition, in a combinational system results in the adjoining of pitches which are not present in the original collection, and thus establishes a new sub-collection; transposition of a set results only in a permutation of the elements. Also, compositional transposition, traditionally, implies contour preservation, a consideration that is, literally, meaningless in defining transposition as a twelve-tone operation, since contour is a function of the registral specification of the elements, and registral choice is as undefined by the structure of a set as is duration, intensity, timbre, or any of the other attributes necessarily associated with a compositional representation of a set; as a result, a set cannot be stated in musical notation without the additional qualification that each pitch sign be taken to signify the total pitch class a member of which it denotes. Since such a qualification only too easily leads to but another confusion of systematic principle with compositional permissive ("a tone may be stated in any octave"), it is both safer and more efficient to represent a twelve-tone set in numerical notation, by an ordered number couple succession, the first member of the couple signifying order position in S ("order number"), the second signifying the "pitch number" of the pitch class. The initial pitch class of S is denoted by the couple (0,0), and is taken as the origin of the coordinate system for both order and pitch numbers, both of which range over the integers 0 — 11 inclusive, each integer appearing once and only once as an order number and a pitch number. In the case of order numbers, this represents the fact that twelve and only twelve pitch classes are involved: in the case of pitch numbers, this is the arithmetical analogue of octave equivalence (congruence mod. 12).[2] In this notation, the set of the Schoenberg Third String Quartet, with registral representation chosen arbitrarily,

Ex. 1

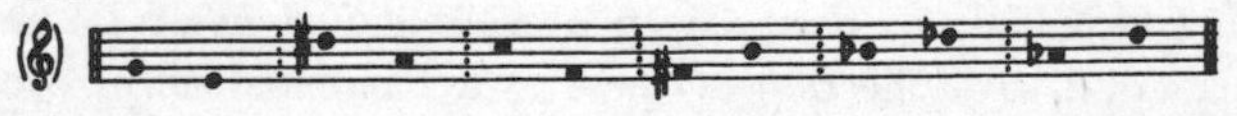

is represented: 0,0; 1,9; 2,8; 3,2; 4,5; 5,10; 6,11; 7,4; 8,3; 9,6; 10,1;

[1] 12! = (12 × 11 × 10 × 9 . . . × 1).

[2] Two numbers, a and b, are said to be "congruent mod. 12" if, and only if, a-b = k.12 where k is an integer (including zero).

11,7. Thus, the succession of differences derived by the subtraction (mod. 12) of a set number from the following set number is the ordered interval succession determined by a set, and each of these interval numbers denotes, accordingly, a class of intervals.

The operation of transposition applied to any set can be represented by adding (mod. 12) an integer, 0 — 11, to each pitch number of the set. Thus, if (a,b) is the couple signifying an element of S, then the transposition is represented by (a,b+t), with t termed the "transposition number." Thus, the transpositional operation (designated: T) is conveniently regarded as an operation on, a permutation of, pitch numbers; for any specified set, it could equally well be regarded as effecting a permutation of order numbers, but the previous characterization corresponds more appropriately to the general conception of transposition.

The totality of twelve transposed sets associated with a given S constitutes a permutation group[3] of order 12; as such it is closed, disjunct with regard to any other collection of sets T derived from a set whose intervallic succession differs from that of any member of this totality. Thus, it constitutes a combinational collection of sets within, not only the totality of all possible sets, but the totality of sets derivable from a given S by the operations of the system.

By virtue of the group structure that it generates, and the additional properties that derive from the commutative and transitive nature of this group, a multitude of attributes necessarily associated with T can be formally deduced. The musical relevance of these attributes can be decided only empirically, of course, but it is my purpose here to examine only a few of those operational invariants (properties of a set

[3] A "group" is a system whose elements (denoted a, b, c . . .), an operation (denoted *), and an equivalence relation (denoted=) satisfy the following properties:

1. Closure: If a, b are elements of the system, then a*b is an element of the system.

2. Associativity: If a, b, c are elements of the system, then (a*b)*c = a*(b*c).

3. Existence of an identity: There is an element of the system, e, such that, for each element of the system (say, d), d*e = e*d = d.

4. Existence of an inverse: For each element of the system (say, d), there exists an element of the system, d-, such that d*d- = d-*d = e.

In interpreting the twelve-tone system as a group, the elements of the group are twelve-tone sets, represented as permutations of pitch or order numbers; the operation is the multiplication of permutations. "S" is the identity element. The "order" of a group is the number of elements of the group.

In addition, the groups presented here have the property of "commutativity": if a, b are elements of the system, then a*b = b*a.

that are preserved under the operation, as well as those relationships between a set and the so-operationally transformed set that inhere in the operation) which may be termed "musical invariants," requiring for their aural recognition merely the ability to perceive pitch class identity and non-identity, and interval class identity and non-identity.

The familiar invariant associated with T is that of preservation of the interval number succession. For all its obviousness, it appears a powerfully cohesive property in the light of the total non-invariance of pitch classes with regard to order; that is, no order, pitch number couple remains fixed under T. Since each t produces a total derangement of the set elements, and the identical intervallic succession, neither of these properties can serve as the bases of differentiation, in the search for possible criteria for the compositional hierarchization of transpositions. Similarly, every value of t defines a regular permutation, but an invariant basis for differentiation appears with the recognition that complementary t's (numbers whose sum is 0, mod. 12), and only such t's, produce inverse permutations, of equal order. Beyond the immediate boundary conditions on the intervallic structure of a set inferrable from this fact, a consequential musical property follows from the further fact that inverse permutations produce the same number of order inversions. This measure of the extent of order rearrangement of the pitch classes can be described most easily by, for the moment, regarding T as an operation on the order numbers of S; an order inversion is each relation among pairs of order numbers that violates the normal ascending relation among order numbers in S. For example, in the set of Ex. 1, the application of, let us say, t = 4 to the set produces the following order number succession: 7, 10, 0, 9, 1,3,8,2,11,5,4,6. The complementary t (t = 8) produces the order number succession: 2,4,7,5,10,9,11,0,6,3,1,8. The number of order inversions produced by each is 32.

Complementary t's produce the same number of pitch adjacencies with regard to S, both ordered adjacencies and reversed adjacencies. (This condition of adjacency is imposed merely in the light of the simplest compositional exploitation of this property, which is immediately extensible to pairs of pitch classes associated with any distribution of order numbers.) If a set possesses successive pitch classes represented by pitch numbers a and b, and successive pitch classes represented by pitch numbers c and d (c may or may not be equal to b, and similarly for d and a), and if b — a = d — c, then there is a t such that a + t = c, and b + t = d, so that under t, a and b are associated with the original order numbers of c and d, and it then follows that under 12 — t, c and d are associated with the original order numbers of a and b. So, too, for reversed adjacencies, represented in the set by complementary intervals. The intervallic structure of S, then, determines the number of adjacencies preserved under a particular t and its complement, since this number is a function of the multiplicity of and relative pitch placement of the identical and complementary interval numbers in S. Consider the set of Ex. 1: the interval succession determined by disjunct dyads is 9,6,5,5,3,6. The interval between the identical 5's is 6, between the complementary intervals 9 and 3 is also 6, and interval 6 is its own complement. So, under the application of t = 6:

the pitch content of disjunct dyads is preserved, and Ex. 2 can thus be regarded as a permutation of the dyads of Ex. 1; if the succession of dyads in Ex. 1 be numbered 1 — 6 inclusive, then those in Ex. 2 are in the order 5,2,4,3,1,6. In the usual cyclic notation, the permutation is (1 5) (3 4). This demonstrates an immediate means of extending serial transformation to compounds of serial elements; I shall return to this aspect of the example later, but it should not be overlooked that in this possibility of holding a pair of pitch classes (as opposed to a pitch class) fixed with regard to order and pitch content, there is immanent the extension to the fixed content trichord, tetrachord, hexachord, etc., or, in other words, to the combinatorial set.

One more property of complementarily transposed sets should be indicated. This involves any segment of S (by segment is meant any number of successive set elements, although the property holds equally for any selection of elements, non-consecutive as well as consecutive), and the corresponding segments of any transposition of the set and the complementary transposition. For example, consider the first seven elements of Ex. 1, and the corresponding elements of transpositions with t = 2 and t = 10:

Considered with regard to this segment of Ex. 1, both segments 3a and 3b have the same number of pitch classes in common with it: four.

But, in addition, the pattern of intersection in terms of order numbers of 3a with regard to 1 is: 0,1,2,5; the pattern of intersection of 1 with regard to 3b is similarly: 0,1,2,5. The actual pitch classes involved, naturally, are not necessarily identical, and are not in the present case. This operational invariant resulting from complementary transposition is not only of obvious rhythmic and functional significance compositionally, but of essential systematic consequence in the theory of general combinatoriality, aggregate structure, and the resultant means of hierarchization of set segments.

The importance of transpositional complementation alone would serve to suggest the systematic operation of inversion (designated: I), which is definable as complementation mod. 12 of each pitch number of S, as opposed to complementation of the t applied to all pitch numbers of S. Given a set element (a,b), I transforms it into (a,12 — b), or, more generally (a,(12 — b) + t), since T is applicable uniquely to the inverted set; with relation to the complex of sets generated by T, the inverted set assumes the local role of S. I and T commute only to within complementation; therefore, the order of operations must be specified, and I shall assume throughout this discussion that T is applied after I (IT).

At this point, it is appropriate to consider comparable definitions of the remaining operations of the system, which reveal that retrogression (designated: R) can be regarded as affecting complementation of order numbers: (a,b) is transformed into (11 — a, b); therefore RI (or the reverse, since the operations commute) merely involves the simultaneous application of both complementation operations: (a,b) is transformed into (11 — a, 12 — b). As in the case of I, t's are applicable to the set numbers.

The presentation of the permutations of S defined by these operations, mod. transposition (in other words, this representation is independent of the operation of transposition), in the usual group multiplication table, with multiplication permutations as the group operation, and S denoting the identity permutation:[4]

S	I	R	RI
I	S	RI	R
R	RI	S	I
RI	R	I	S

[4] The group table is read by choosing an element in the first column and the element with which it is to be multiplied in the first row; the result of this multiplication is found at the intersection of the row of the first and the column of the second.

reveals, first of all, that this collection of permutations is an instance of a group, and as such possesses the property of closure, thus assuring another combinational aspect of the system in the large, since the collection of sets determined by these permutations is disjunct with regard to any so determined collection of sets one of whose sets is not a member of this collection, and is identical with a collection one of whose members is.

The revealed symmetry properties indicate the hazardous connotations of such terms as "basic" or "original" set to denote other than a set form norm decided upon purely on the basis of contextual considerations (temporal priority, for example), since such terms cannot designate any attribute of set structure in a general sense, either from a standpoint of internal properties or of relation to other set forms. Similarly, the fact that the period of each of the permutations is 2 should, in itself, dispel once and for all those futile attempts to "equate" these operations with tonal functions.

A vast literature of group theory supplies necessary properties of such a structure, and it is not without extra-musical interest that this particular group of permutations is an instance of a familiar group structure, the so-called "four-group."

The twelve-tone system, as system, is indeed "simple." It is simple in its principles of formation and transformation, but enormously complex and deep in its ramifications, in the necessary inferences that can be drawn from these principles, for it is of the formal model of which it is an exemplification that Hermann Weyl has said: "From these insignificant looking assumptions springs an abundance of profound relationships; and mathematics offers an astounding variety of different interpretations of this simple axiom system."[5]

Inversion, in the traditional sense, implies inversion of contour. In the twelve-tone system inversion, like transposition, cannot be characterized in terms of registral considerations, but merely as that permutation of pitch class numbers (or, for particular purposes, of order numbers) which results from the substitution of complementary pitch numbers in S; it follows that there is an accompanying substitution of a succession of complementary intervals for the interval succession of S.

Even more, perhaps, than in the case of T, I must derive its "justification" from its associated musical invariants. It must be emphasized

[5] *Philosophy of Mathematics and Natural Science,* Princeton, 1949, p. 28.

that, although invariants are associated necessarily with the operations in question, the degree to which they are projected explicitly in compositional terms depends upon the emphasis they receive from other musical components: rhythm, dynamics, register, phrasing, timbre, etc. Conversely, the desire for the compositional exploitation of these fundamental properties may be regarded as, at least, a partial determinant of the compositional characteristics imposed on these components.

Consider the simplest inversional invariant: if (a,b) of S is transformed by IT into the corresponding order element (a,(12 — b) + t), where (12 — b) + t may or may not be equal to b, then, corresponding to (c,(12 — b) + t) of S is (c,b). This property, as may be observed by reference to our examples, is possessed also by transposition when t = 6; it holds for all t's applied to the inversion.

Again, the cyclic representation of the pitch class permutations effected by IT shows that all even t's produce similar permutations of six cycles of two elements each (thus, regular permutations), while odd t's produce similar permutations of five two-element cycles and two unit cycles. So, although complementary t's still produce similar permutations, this is merely because they are either both even or both odd. Odd values of t, then, determine six dyadic pitch classes between elements of the same order number in I related sets, and even values of t determine five such dyadic classes, and two single-element classes. These latter represent set elements whose order number, pitch number couple remains unchanged under IT. It is for this reason that a necessary condition for hexachordal inversional combinatoriality is that the sum of the set numbers of the same order number in the I related sets be odd. The pitch number of an element so fixed is equal to one half of t; thus, the two such fixed elements associated with a given even t are unique, and are tritone related (since 12/2 = 6).

In addition to this partition of the elements of inversionally related sets into pitch classes, the IT operation also effects a categorization into interval classes. Since the intervals between pitch classes of the same order number in I related sets are either all even or all odd, and — thus — each interval occurs exactly twice, it can be shown that pitch classes in S whose pitch numbers differ by 6 are associated with the same interval determined by the element of the same order number in the I related set.

The largely "note against note" presentation of the canon in the second movement of Webern's Variations for Piano places these characteristics in the foreground. The initially stated, I related forms of the set (Ex. 4a):

Ex. 4

since t = 2 (taking the lower of the two sets as the reference "prime" set), hold (1,1) and (11,7) fixed. Since the first hexachord of S contains no tritone related pitches, there is no repetition of pitch dyads formed by elements of the same order number, so that, if the first succession of six dyads is numbered 1,2,3,4,5,6, then the following succession is a permutation of these: 6,4,1,5,3,2. As in the Schoenberg example, although in a different manner, complexes of pitch elements become, themselves, subjected to serial permutation.

The continuation of this canon demonstrates the compositional use of another invariant. By choosing, as the initial pitches (or, as any pitches of the same order number, since the sums of the pitch numbers of such pairs are equal) of the T forms of the S and the I related set, elements the sum of whose pitch numbers, with regard to the original reference point "g#" = (0,0), is equal to the original t = 2, the pitch dyads resulting are identical with those created in the first inversional juxtaposition. The recurrence of repeated "a's" is merely one manifestation of this general property. See Ex. 4b. Therefore, for each first element of a set, there is one and only one choice of the first element of the I related set which holds the pitch dyads so fixed with regard to a pre-defined norm. (In the light of the previous discussion, it is of interest to point out that an equivalent statement of this condition is that the initial I related forms be transposed by complementary values of t.) Webern chooses four of these twelve possibilities to determine the pitch levels of the successive sections of the movement; the first and last pitches of the I related sets which provide the pitch content of the third and fourth sections of the work are shown in Ex. 4c. The first movement of Webern's Quartet, Op. 22, employs the same procedure in a more elaborate and extended manner.

The more common and traditional procedure of "totally transposing" such a section — in my terms, the applying of the same t to both simultaneously stated forms — preserves the interval succession but not (except the single case where t = 6) the fixed pitch dyads: the procedure under discussion here permutes the interval succession while retaining the pitch content of the dyads.

If we number the dyads of the first section from 1 - 12 inclusive, the second section yields a permutation corresponding exactly to the permutation of order numbers that results from applying t = 5 to the upper set, or — equivalently — t = 7 to the lower set, and — of course — correspondingly with the third and fourth sections. Thus, all the properties associated with the application of T to S are translatable into properties of permutations of dyads between I related sets.

Webern's particular choice of transpositions appears to be related primarily to concerns of compositional duration and external design. The transpositional choice for the second section makes possible a final dyad for this section which is pitch identical with the initial dyad of the movement, but with pitch components reversed as to set membership. The repeat of these first two sections is founded on this identity. The third section is transpositionally determined by exact analogy with the second section, through the "double function" of the final dyad of the preceding section. But the continuation of this basis of choice, since the interval between the first and last elements of the set is prime to 12, would carry the work through all possible twelve jointly determined transpositions before returning to the first dyad in its original disposition. So, the fourth section employs the principle of interchange, already introduced into the work by the repeat of the first two sections. The fourth section thus effects a return to the first dyad of the movement, while the repeat of the third and fourth sections as a unit results in another interchange, necessarily the exact reverse of the interchange resulting from the first repeat.

Closely related to these invariants is the property: if (a,b) and (a + 1,c) are two successive elements of S (the provision of succession is, actually, unnecessary, but is introduced here for purposes of simplicity), and (d,e) is an element of an I related set (where d may or may not be identical with a or a = 1, and e may or may not be identical with b or c), then the intervallic succession b — e, c — e is identical with the succession g — f, h — f, defined by d,f of the initial set, and a,g and a + 1, h of the I related set. In the *Contrapunctus Secundus* of the *Quaderno Musicale di Annalibera,* which is in many structural respects closely similar to the Webern movement just discussed, Dallapiccola uses this property in the second half of the piece as a means of unfolding the same intervallic progression by the two canonic parts, while reversing their relation of temporal priority. This property, as well as the fixed dyad property, is particularly significant as a harmonic factor when extended to include more than two simultaneously stated, I related sets.

As in the case of T, conditions for the retention of pitch adjacencies under IT are statable easily and fully. However, I merely shall return to Ex. 1, and examine the result of applying IT with $t = 3$, and $t = 9$.

Ex. 5

The pitch content of disjunct dyads is preserved, and the permutations of these dyads under I for $t = 3$ is (1 5) (2 6), and for $t = 9$ is (2 6) (3 4). Taken together with the identity permutation and the permutation under $t = 6$, this group of permutations leaves each dyad twice fixed with regard to order, once with its component elements in the order defined by S, and once with the elements reversed; of the four occurrences of each dyad, two maintain the order of elements defined by S, and two reverse this order. More generally, if we denote by A the identity permutation of the dyads, by B the permutation on the dyads effected by $t = 6$, by C and D the permutations effected by IT with t equal respectively to 3 and 6, the multiplication table for this group of permutations is:

A	B	C	D
B	A	D	C
C	D	A	B
D	C	B	A

This group is isomorphic with that formed by the permutations representing the identity, I, R, RI operations of the system.

Finally, the familiar phrase: "the identification of the horizontal with the vertical," implies much more than a mere compositional prescriptive with regard to the spatial distribution of the elements of a set when it is realized that adjacent pitch elements of a set become elements of the same order number in I related sets, when these sets are so chosen that the sum of the pitch numbers of any two elements of the same order number is equal to the sum of the pitch numbers of the originally adjacent elements.

Space does not permit a consideration of invariance under R and RI. However, it must be pointed out that the traditional conception of retrogression as effecting the temporal reversal of pitches constitutes neither a meaningful description nor a "justification" for its position in the twelve-tone system. For, even with registral considerations disregarded, this characteristic is associated with but one transpositional level of the retrograde; but all transpositional levels of the retrograde present the intervallic succession of the *inversion* in reversed order, while — necessarily — the retrograde-inversion forms present the intervallic succession of the *prime* (S) in reversed order. Thus, the RI forms, often regarded as the aurally most unrealistic transformations, because the operation is viewed as applied to pitch succession rather than to interval succession, require for the perception of their relation to S merely the ability to identify interval classes. In this important sense, the RI forms can be regarded as the most closely related to S, and are so employed often by Schoenberg in his compositional, "thematic" presentation of successive set forms: see, for example, the Variations for Orchestra, the third movement of the Fourth String Quartet, and the Piano Concerto. In the pitch class order, interval class order duality between retrograde and retrograde-inverted related sets reside many of the most important properties of such transformations.

Even so incomplete and informal a discussion of so small a number of the invariants attending the operations of the system indicates, I hope, something of the essential importance of this subject, analytically in the "rational reconstruction" of compositions, and compositionally in comprehending and mastering the materials of the system. If I have led the discussion more in the direction of those aspects which suggest the "macrocosmically" combinational features of this basically permutational system, I could have — with equal appropriateness and the same means — examined the "microcosmically" combinational features (particularly what are termed in group theory "imprimitive systems"), set structure (particularly with regard to redundancy properties), combinatoriality, generalized partitioning, derivation, sequence theory, and related questions.

Certainly, any conjectures about "generalized" serialism must confront the problem as to whether such alleged generalizations result in a maintenance, an increase, or a decrease, of the number and scope of such invariants, and whether the apparent "freedom" of such "generalizations" does not, in a deeper sense, reduce structural resources rather than augment them.

Likewise, I would insist that a necessary condition for the application of the permutational operations of the twelve-tone system to orderable non-pitch elements is that the rules of correlation be so arrived at that these invariants, which are necessary consequences of the pitch class nature of the system, be susceptible to musically meaningful interpretations in these other, perhaps significantly dissimilar, domains.

In conclusion, I can state only, without hoping to have done more than intimate the bases for such a statement, that an "exhaustion" of the resources of the twelve-tone system in the relevant future is not only unforseeable, but unthinkable. I trust I have begun to document, and will be given the opportunity in the future to further document, the statement that, in its vastness of structural means, its flexibility, and its precision, the twelve-tone system cedes nothing to any musical system of the past or present that has engaged the mind of musical man.

Music Titles in The Norton Library

Bekker, Paul *The Orchestra* N219

Broder, Nathan, EDITOR *The Great Operas of Mozart* N256

Bukofzer, Manfred F. *Studies in Medieval and Renaissance Music* N241

Copland, Aaron *Copland on Music* N198

David, Hans T. and Arthur Mendel, EDITORS *The Bach Reader* N259

Einstein, Alfred *Essays on Music* N177

Fux, Johann J. *The Study of Counterpoint* (*Gradus Ad Parnassum*) Translated and edited by Alfred Mann N277

Hutchings, A. J. B. *The Baroque Concerto* N315

Ives, Charles *Essays Before a Sonata and Other Writings* Selected and edited by Howard Boatwright N244

Lang, Paul Henry, EDITOR *The Creative World of Mozart* N218

Lang, Paul Henry, EDITOR *Stravinsky:* A New Appraisal of His Music N199

Lang, Paul Henry, EDITOR *Problems of Modern Music* N115

Moore, Douglas *A Guide to Musical Styles:* From Madrigal to Modern Music N200

Moore, Douglas *Listening to Music* N130

Pincherle, Marc *Vivaldi: Genius of the Baroque* N168

Reeves, James, EDITOR *The Idiom of the People* One hundred and fifteen folk songs chosen from the manuscripts of Cecil Sharp N289

Sachs, Curt *World History of the Dance* N209

Stravinsky, Igor *An Autobiography* N161

Toye, Francis *Rossini: A Study in Tragi-Comedy* N192

Walter, Bruno *Of Music and Music-Making* N242

Westrup, J. A., and F. Ll. Harrison *The New College Encyclopedia of Music* N273

Norton / Haydn Society Records

A TREASURY OF EARLY MUSIC

Four 12-inch 33⅓ RPM long-play records to supplement Parrish's *A Treasury of Early Music.* Monaural and Stereophonic.

Parrish's *A Treasury of Early Music.* Monaural and Stereo.

Record 1 *Music of the Middle Ages*
Examples 1 through 12

Record 2 *Music of the Ars Nova and the Renaissance*
Examples 13 through 28

Record 3 *Music of the Renaissance and Baroque*
Examples 29 through 41

Record 4 *Music of the Baroque*
Examples 42 through 50

MASTERPIECES OF MUSIC BEFORE 1750

Three 12-inch 33⅓ RPM long-play records to supplement Parrish and Ohl, *Masterpieces of Music Before 1750.* Monaural.

Record 1 *Gregorian Chant to the 16th Century*
Examples 1 through 22

Record 2 *The 16th and 17th Centuries*
Examples 23 through 36

Record 3 *The 17th and 18th Centuries*
Examples 37 through 50